Word Puzzles

Catherine Veitch

OXFORD
UNIVERSITY PRESS

For Dad, who put up with me during a month of intense puzzle writing, and who was always on hand to solve copious puzzles — CV

OXFORD
UNIVERSITY PRESS

Great Clarendon Street, Oxford, OX2 6DP, United Kingdom

Oxford University Press is a department of the University of Oxford. It furthers the University's objective of excellence in research, scholarship, and education by publishing worldwide. Oxford is a registered trade mark of Oxford University Press in the UK and in certain other countries

Author: Catherine Veitch

The moral rights of the author have been asserted

First published in 2019

British Library Cataloguing in Publication Data
Data available

978-0-19-276955-8

10 9 8 7 6 5

Paper used in the production of this book is a natural, recyclable product made from wood grown in sustainable forests. The manufacturing process conforms to the environmental regulations of the country of origin.

Printed in China

Acknowledgements

Cover illustrations by Holly Fulbrook
Page make-up and illustrations by James Hunter

Hi Puzzle Fan,

Are you ready to test your word power? This book is bursting with riddles, anagrams, picture puzzles, crosswords, word searches and word fits. Sharpen your pencil and let's kick-start your brain with these word-puzzle challenges.

Be a puzzle detective and…

- look for hidden words and missing letters
- find your way around mazes
- crack the codes
- unscramble letters
- and solve the clues.

Along the way you will meet some interesting characters, giggle at rib-tickling jokes and learn some fascinating facts.

How to use this book

In this book there are three sections of puzzles – warm-up, intermediate and tricky. They get more challenging as you progress through the book.

Follow the simple introduction at the start of each puzzle and use a pencil in case you need to rub anything out. Try the quick quiz at the end of each section to see how much you remember and add up your score to discover your puzzle power.

By the end of the book you will have fine-tuned your spelling, brushed up on your grammar and boosted your vocabulary. That means increased word power, too!

You can find the answers at the back of the book, but don't look until you have completed each puzzle section! A notepad is included on some pages in case you need space to help you work out the answer.

We've put in some Puzzle Pointers to give you a clue so look out for the jigsaw symbol.

So what are you waiting for? Let's get going on some word-puzzle challenges...

Warm-up puzzles

1 Just joking!

Find the letters that appear more than four times in box 1, and more than five times in box 2. Then unscramble the letters to spell out the answer to the joke. Write the answer in the boxes.

Which athlete is warm in winter?

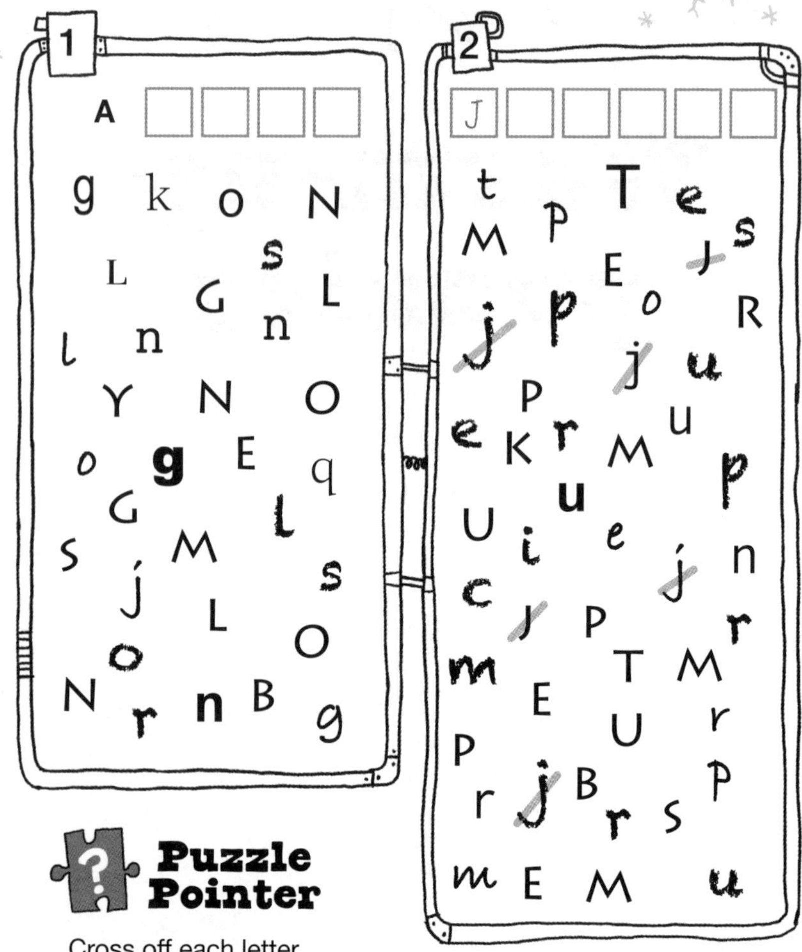

Puzzle Pointer

Cross off each letter as you count it.

2 Raining bats and frogs!

Warm-up

It rains a lot in the rainforest, but that doesn't put off the inhabitants! Find and cross off all the rainforest creatures in the word search. They are written forwards, backwards, up, down or diagonally. Then write the remaining letters, in order, in the answer boxes to spell out a creature you wouldn't want to touch.

Watch out! The word **ant** also appears in the word tar**ant**ula. Look for another ant.

a	l	u	t	n	a	r	a	t	p
r	r	a	e	t	o	a	d	c	o
c	b	m	i	g	o	r	f	h	c
h	s	o	a	t	r	n	r	a	o
e	w	a	n	d	r	e	p	m	l
r	r	a	r	o	i	y	t	e	o
f	i	w	c	s	b	l	f	l	b
i	p	d	r	a	z	i	l	e	u
s	a	a	r	r	m	o	g	o	s
h	t	a	d	n	o	c	a	n	a

anaconda
ant
archerfish
armadillo
bat
capybara
chameleon
colobus
egret
frog
lizard
macaw
tapir
tarantula
tarsier
toad

3 Pick up pens

Warm-up

Find out how Talia has performed in drama. Write the letter from each pen, starting with the pen on the top of the pile, to spell out the missing word on Talia's report.

4 The tale of Charlie Crumb

The poet has got in a muddle and some words are wrong. Choose the correct word from the list of words that rhymes with each incorrect word, and write it on the line. There are more words here than you need, so pick carefully!

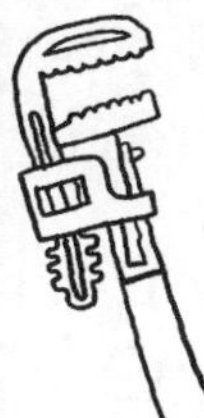

runner	shout	crews	fine
gone	fend	know	doubt
sum	numb	Rhine	plumber
cruise	no	friend	John

There once was a plumber to everyone,
Who went by the name of Charlie Crumb.
One day Charlie saw his good friend ~~Von~~ ____________ ,
Who spotted that Charlie was feeling ~~tum~~ ____________ .

Charlie had finished with sinks and loos,
And was looking forward to getting out.
But as he was leaving for his world ~~who's~~ ____________ ,
He wasn't so sure and began to ~~trout~~ ____________ .

"I'm scared," said Charlie to his good ~~send~~ ____________ .
"Can I do it? I don't really ~~toe~~ ____________ ,
Problems in houses are what I mend."
"Relax," said John. "And just take it slow."

So Charlie packed his bags for summer,
And went off to sail along the ~~dine~~ ____________ .
And ever since he's been a ~~drummer~~ ____________ ,
Happily working for a big cruise line.

5 Cheeky chef

Warm-up

Cheeky chef Chas will only cook using foods **beginning** with the letters **ch**. Can you circle ten foods in the food spiral that Chas can cook with?

Puzzle Pointer

Some incorrect words have been thrown in, so don't get caught out! Remember the food needs to **begin** with **ch**.

6 Shocking selfie

What do you call it when a prisoner takes their own mugshot? A **cell**fie!

Join the dots in descending alphabetical order from z to a, to reveal this prisoner's cellfie.

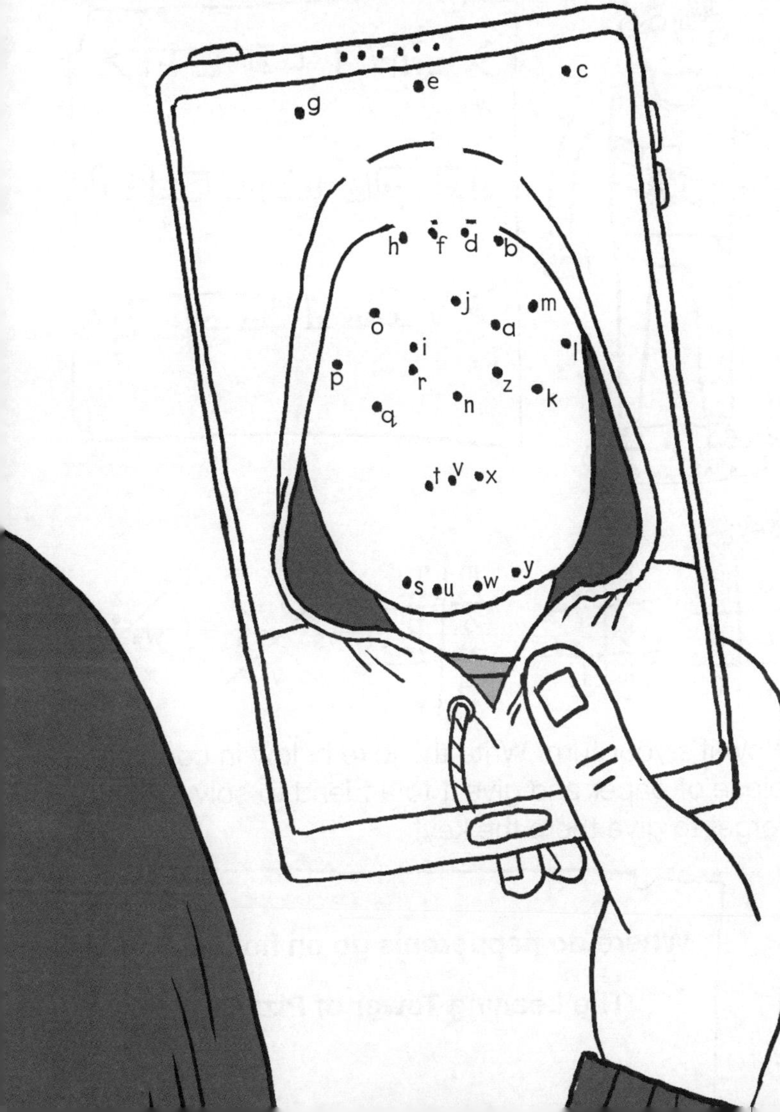

7 Message in a bottle

Dexter has found a message in a bottle that has washed up on the shore, but it's all in code. Using the key, how quickly can you crack the code and work out what it says?

Key:

a b c d e f

g h i j k l

m n o p q r

s t u v

w x y z

Now it's your turn. Write the joke below in code on a piece of paper and give it to a friend to solve. Don't forget to give them the key!

Where do pepperonis go on holiday?

The Leaning Tower of Pizza!

Beside the seashore

How quickly can you fit all the sea words into the grid?

barnacle
lobster
periwinkle
scallop
seaweed
shrimp
starfish

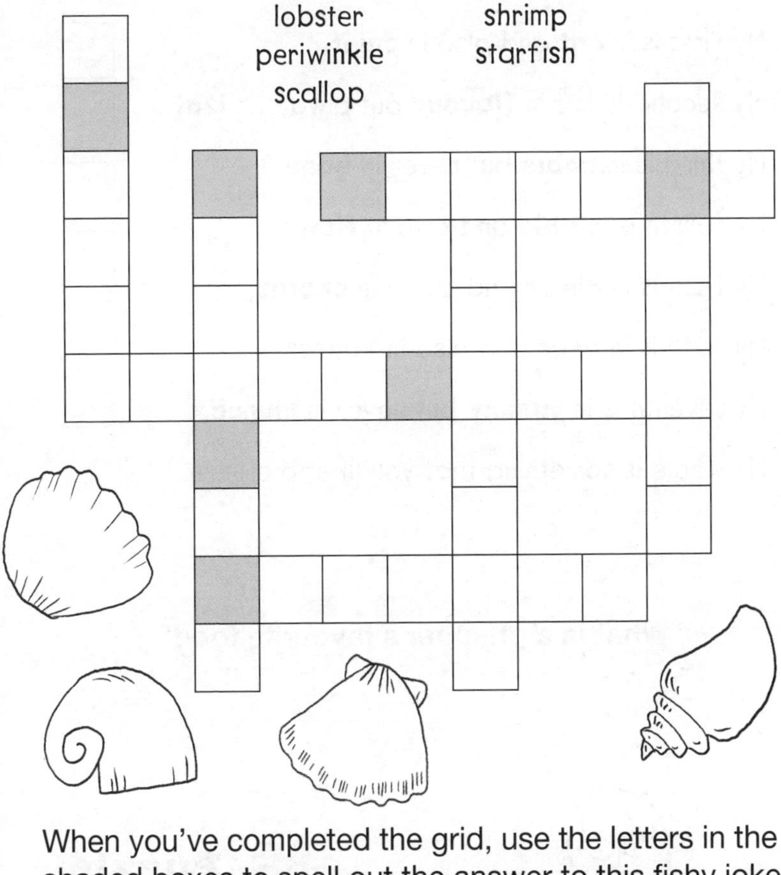

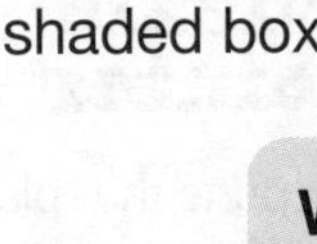

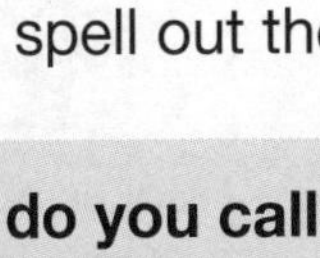

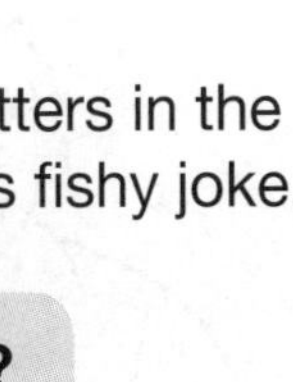

When you've completed the grid, use the letters in the shaded boxes to spell out the answer to this fishy joke.

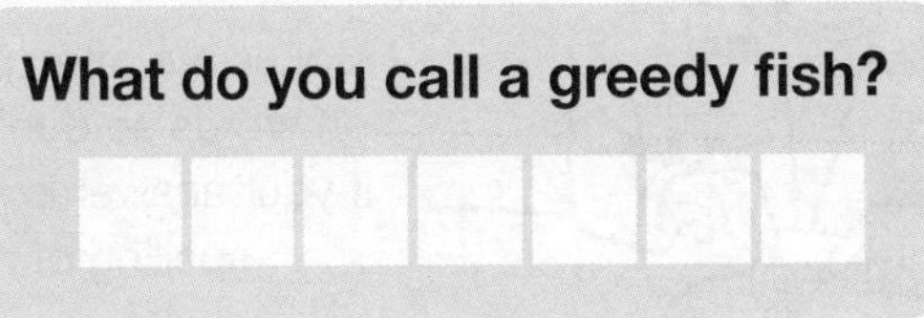

Warm-up

9 What am I 1?

Warm-up

Read the riddle and work out the seven-letter word that is the answer to the joke.

My first is in **cat** and also in **chief**,
My second is not in **flavour** but always in **leaf**.
My third is in **noble** but never in **bone**,
My fourth is in **able** and also in **flown**.
My fifth is in **cheer** and never in **chorus**,
My sixth is in **deer** and also in **Taurus**.
My seventh is in **yummy** but never in **munch**,
My whole is something that you like to crunch.

What is a prisoner's favourite food?

Jokes are often puns that play on words so don't be surprised if your answer is not the correct spelling of the word.

10 Tiny trail

Help the little cygnet find the way to his parent. He can only step on rectangles containing words that mean the same as *tiny* and he can only move up, right, left or down one rectangle at a time. The cygnet's first move is shown.

tiny →	small	jumbo	whopping
enormous	minute	huge	vast
big	wee	little	miniscule
tremendous	monstrous	oversize	teeny
grand	mini	teeny-weeny	microscopic
great	dinky	bumper	towering
massive	pocket-sized	miniature	petite

11 Word square 1

How many words of **four or more** letters can you make using the letters in this word square? Names and plurals don't count. Can you spot a nine-letter word?

a	l	c
o	m	e
h	e	n

Puzzle Pointer

Look for common letter combinations, such as **me** or **ea**, and go through the rest of the letters to see if any will combine with these letters to make a word.

ache

Puzzle Pointer

The nine-letter word is a colour-changing reptile.

Warm-up

12 Solar system search

Can you find and cross off the solar system words in this word search faster than an exploding star? The words can be written forwards, backwards, up, down or diagonally.

comet
Earth
Jupiter
Mars
Mercury
moon
Neptune
star
Uranus
Venus

		t	e	m	o	c	
	s	u	n	a	r	u	
	c	o	e	m	a	e	s
t	j	u	p	i	t	e	r
e	a	r	t	h	s	b	a
o	y	r	u	c	r	e	m
	o	k	n	o	o	m	
		v	e	n	u	s	

When you've finished the word search, write the leftover letters, in order, in the boxes below to spell out the answer to this space joke.

What is a planet's favourite thing to read?

A ☐☐☐☐☐ ☐☐☐☐!

13 Dazzle Dance Show

Here are the contestants for the Dazzle Dance Show. In all the excitement, the judges have forgotten their words.

Can you fill in the missing words to complete the similes in each sentence to finish what the judges had to say?

You were full of drama like ______________________________ .

It was as graceful as ______________________________ .

It was so slow like you were ______________________________ .

It was as scary as ______________________________ .

It was as entertaining as ______________________________ .

You were as quick as ______________________________ .

stuck in mud **a beautiful swan** **a diva**

a rollercoaster ride **lightning** **a clown**

Pretend you are a judge. Write a sentence including a simile about each contestant. Will you give any contestants full marks?

____

____

____

____

____

____

14 Picture puzzle 1

Warm-up

Name the pictures and follow the instructions to delete and add letters, to spell out a joke.

?

!

15 Letter trail

Follow the trail of each skier down the slope and collect the letters. Then unscramble the letters for each skier to spell out the number of seconds it took to get to the bottom. The skier who took the least time is the winner. Who won the race?

Warm-up

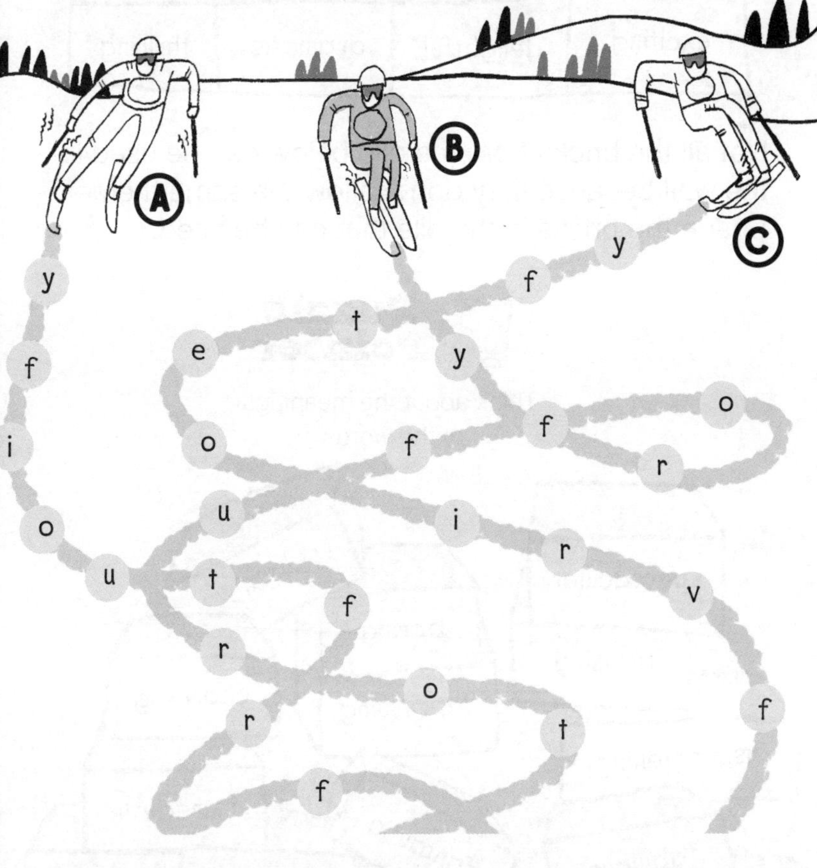

Skier A took ______________________ seconds.

Skier B took ______________________ seconds.

Skier C took ______________________ seconds.

16 Word wall 1

Can you spot a theme to the words in this wall?

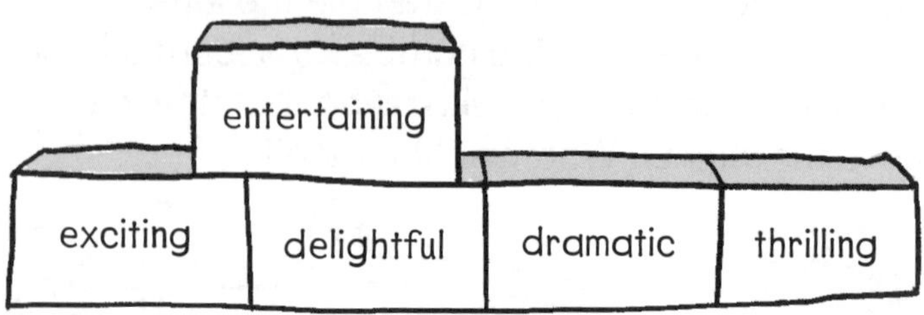

Not all the bricks from the pile below can be used in the wall because they don't follow the same theme. Shade the bricks in the pile that can be used.

Think about the meanings of the words.

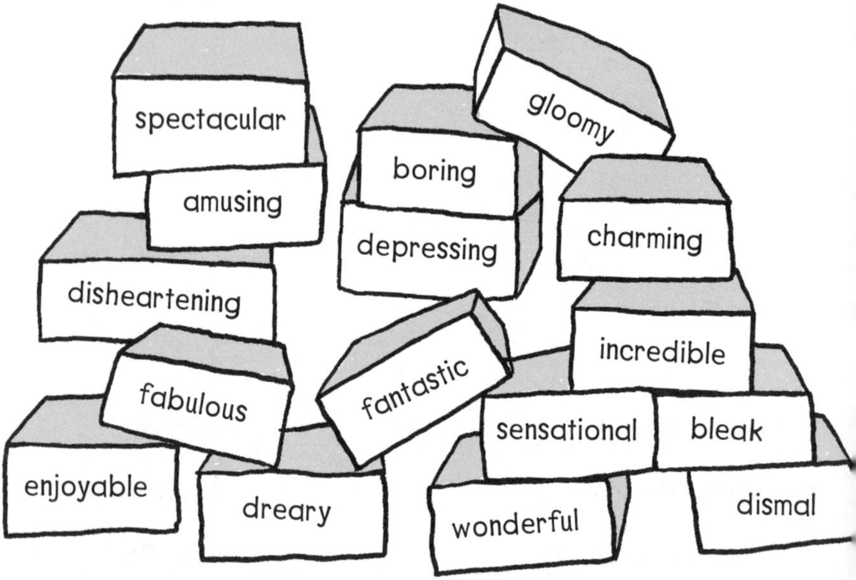

spectacular
amusing
boring
gloomy
depressing
charming
disheartening
incredible
fabulous
fantastic
sensational
bleak
enjoyable
dreary
wonderful
dismal

17 The big picture

How quickly can you guess the well-known expressions? Say exactly what you see, and write your answers in the boxes. The first one has been done for you.

1. 

2. 

3. 

4. 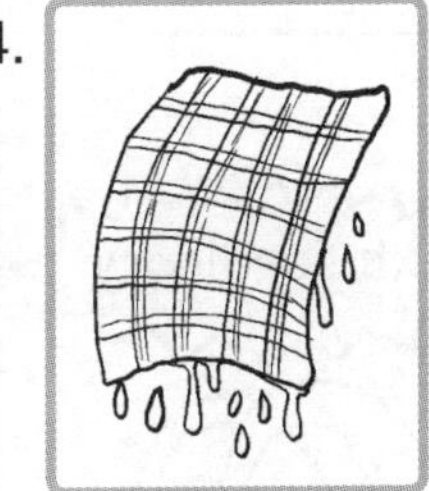

5. 

6. 

1. Couch potato
  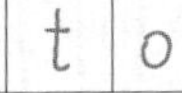

2. A

3.

4. A

5. I'll
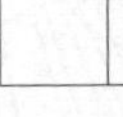

6. The
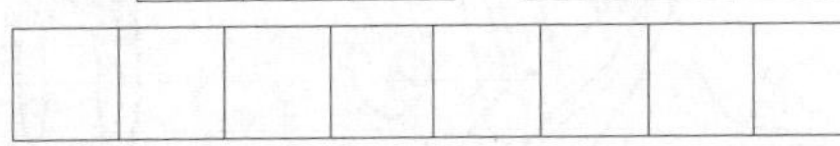

18 Jupiter's stars

Inhabitants of the solar system have assembled on Jupiter for their annual talent competition. Here are the eight finalists. Read what the judges said about each act.

Pretend you are a judge and make up 12 more words that you might say about the contestants. Join one prefix to one root word to make each word. Do not use any hyphens.

Prefixes
super
im
in
dis
out
un

Root words	
cool	patient
appropriate	usual
sonic	ruly
sane	hero
mature	human
like	dated

Warm-up

19 What am I 2?

Read the riddle to work out the ten-letter word that is the answer to the joke.

My first is in **home** and always in **thin**,
My second is in **child** and also in **grin**.
My third is in **loud** but never in **proud**,
My fourth is in **leak** and also in **loud**.
My fifth is in **steam** and always in **chair**,
My sixth is in **creep** and also in **stair**.
My seventh is in **slip** but never in **please**,
My eighth is in **foal** and never in **fleas**.
My ninth is in **umbrella** and also in **shrug**,
My tenth is in **share** and always in **slug**.
Finish the rhyme and work out its glitches,
A mountain to climb will have you in stitches.

What do you call a funny mountain?

_______________ !

Remember that puns don't have to use the correct spelling of the word.

20 Slimy code

Warm-up

Slurpy Seth is cooking up a feast and has a list of the ingredients he needs. But his list is gobbledygook! Can you crack the code to help Slurpy Seth work out what he needs for his recipe?

The letters of a **slimy toad** have jumped in between the words.

You will need:

1. nsolsiem hyatiorasd   nose hairs
2. psilcikmlyetdo taode   ______
3. fsilnigmeyrt woaardt   ______
4. cshloicmoyltaotaed   ______
5. bslluiem tyotnogaude   ______
6. fsilsihm byutropasd   ______

21 Picture this 1

Can you guess the words shown in these illustrations? Unscramble the letters in each root word and choose the correct prefix from below to make each word.

sub super anti

Now draw your own illustration of a word with one of these prefixes. Muddle the letters of its root word and see if a friend can guess the word.

22 Healing words

Warm-up

Match the words in each pyramid to make new compound words. Then unscramble all the first letters of the new words to spell out the name of something the Ancient Egyptians put on their cuts to heal them.

come

over day wear

light life ~~man~~ moon

style under dream ~~yachts~~

yachtsman

____

____

____

____

____

~~air~~

block river

dish ear ~~port~~

phones buster bank washer

airport

____

____

____

____

The Ancient Egyptians used

					y

			a	

.

23 Time to talk

How a character says something changes the meaning of their words. The words below are alternatives to the word **said** that can be used in writing.

"Can you fit all the words in the word grid?" **demanded** the writer. Oops, that sounds too harsh!

"Can you fit all the words in the word grid?" **asked** the writer. That's better… so what are you waiting for?

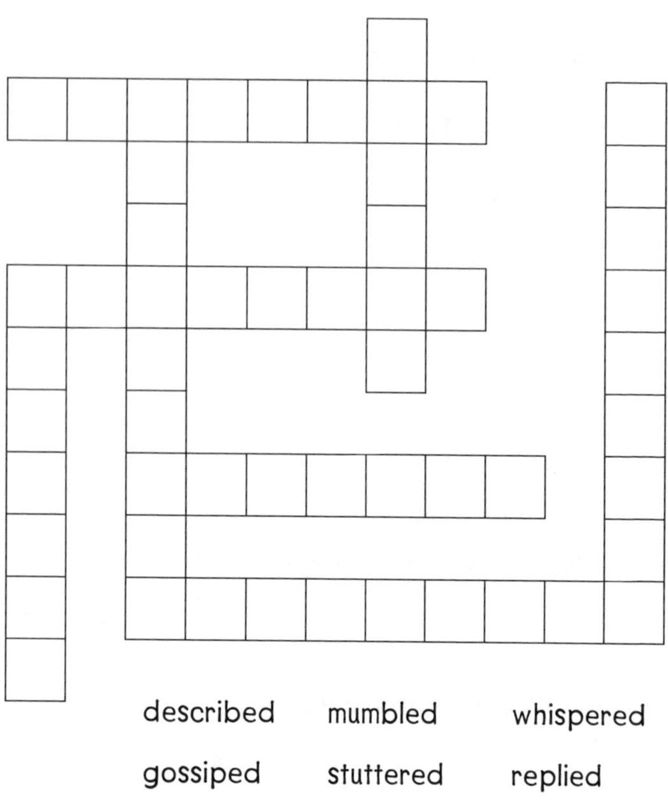

described mumbled whispered
gossiped stuttered replied
muttered teased

Now choose the appropriate word from the word grid and fill in the missing words in these sentences. You can only use each word once.

Warm-up

1. "I'm sorry that I rode your precious bike," __________________ Liam.

2. "I d ... don't think I can climb down as I'm sc ... sc ... ared of heights!" __________________ Amy.

3. "My gorgeous pug is brown, two years old, and called Scotty," __________________ Sasha.

4. "Did you hear that Teddy had his picture taken by the local paper?" __________________ Jess.

5. "It's lovely to see you, too," __________________ Mohammed.

6. "If you're nice to me, I'll let you sit here," __________________ Alice.

7. "Shh, be quiet," __________________ Hideko.

8. "I don't like playing football in the rain," __________________ Alfie.

Some words will fit in more than one sentence. Choose the word that is the most **suitable**.

24 Dominique's boutique

Warm-up

Dominique's boutique is unique as it only sells things **containing** the letters **que** in that order. Dominique is buying more stock. Can you help her decide what to buy by circling ten things in the word spiral that she can sell in her shop?

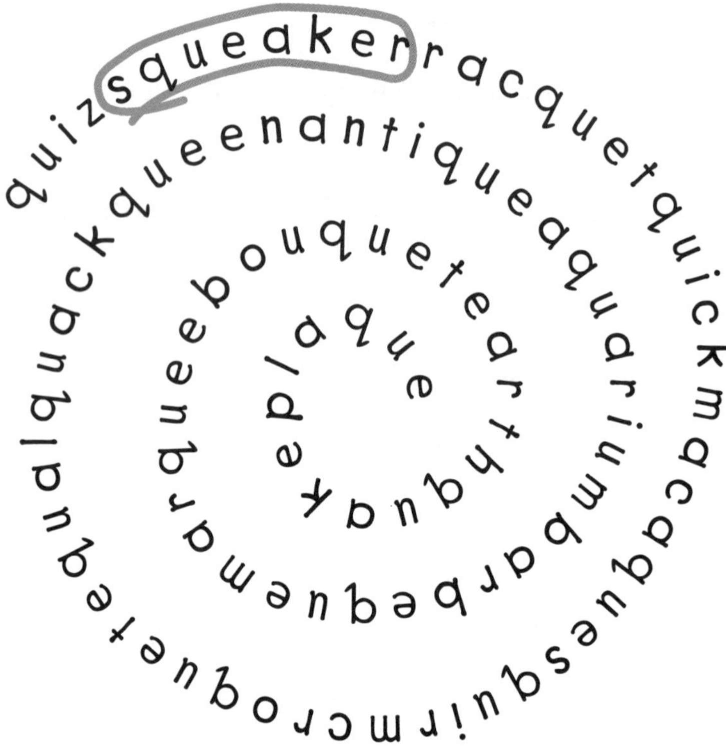

quizsqueakerracquetquickmacaquesquirmcroquetequalquackqueenantiqueaquariumbarbequemarqueebouquetearthquakeplaque

Puzzle Pointer

There are lots of words with the letter **q** in them here, so don't get caught out! Remember it needs to contain all three letters **que** in that order.

Arctic animals

Look at the answers given and try to crack the code to work out the other eight creatures found in the chilly Arctic. Can you guess which name belongs to the strange creature in the illustration? Its tusk is actually one of its teeth!

Puzzle Pointer

Look for a pattern in the letters. Use this pattern to work out the other names.

1. wrauls ______
2. pboelaarr (2 words) ______
3. arlobsast ______
4. bwehlaulgea (2 words) ______
5. Acrfcotxi (2 words) ______
6. nhaarlw ______
7. Epmepnegruoirn (2 words) Emperor penguin
8. pfuifn ______
9. rdeeienr ______
10. Wlesdedaell (2 words) Weddell seal

26 Tongue-tied

Read these tongue-twisters five times, as quickly as you can.

The superior, supersonic submarine was submerged in a salty, subfreezing sea.

The superstitious superstar with super silky strands, swished and swayed in a sassy, superhuman style.

The disagreeable disco diva discovered a disappointing disco dance.

Now make up some tongue-twisters of your own about a submarine, a superstar and a disco diva. Try to include words beginning with **s** and **d**.

You could include some of these words:

sublime	suspicious	superpower
substantial	superb	supervision
subtle	supertanker	disguise
supercool	superior	disgusting

27 Music trail

Follow the trail of the musician's guitar lead to collect some letters. Write down the letters in order in the notepad. Then circle every fourth letter to spell out the answer to the joke.

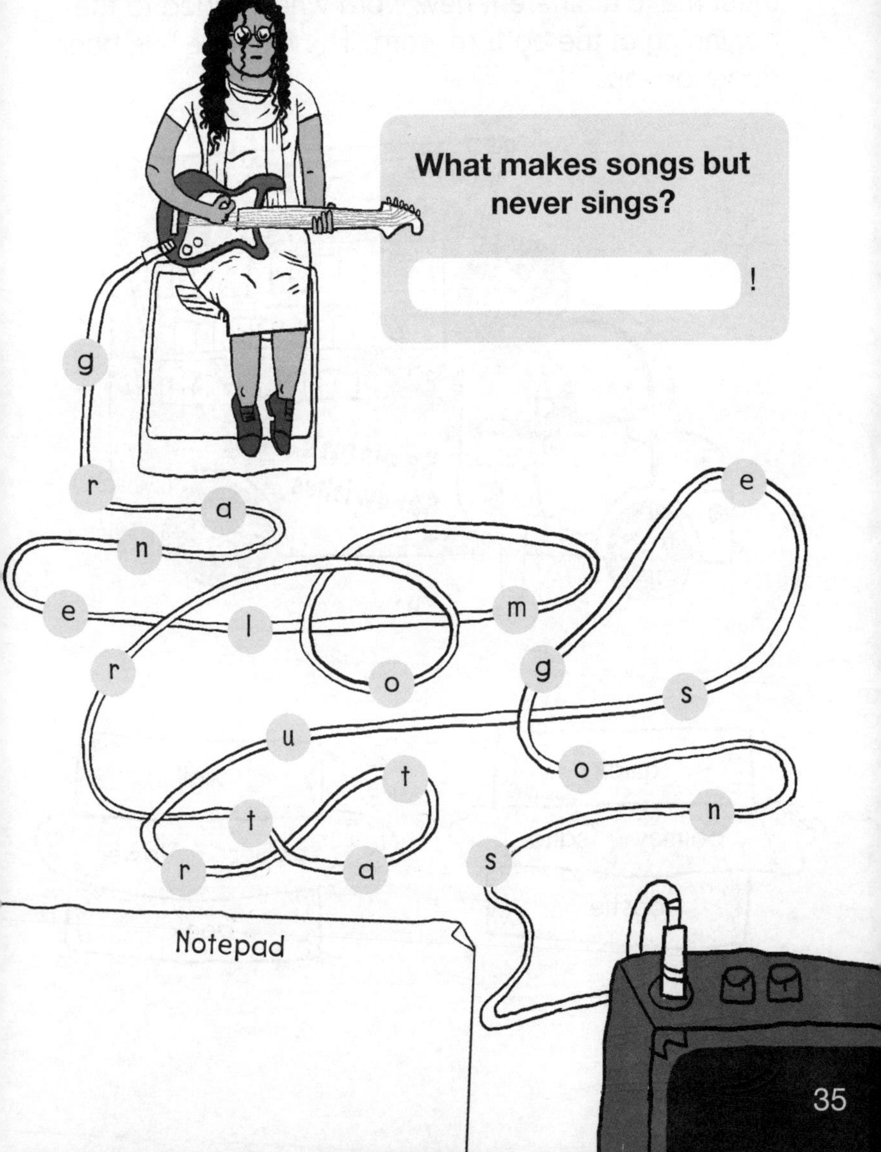

28 Word sandwiches 1

Warm-up

Samson has forgotten to put the fillings in his word sandwiches. Can you circle the correct word filling for each sandwich? The filling must make a new word when added to the end of the top word, and it must make a different new word when added to the beginning of the bottom word. The first one has been done for you.

1.
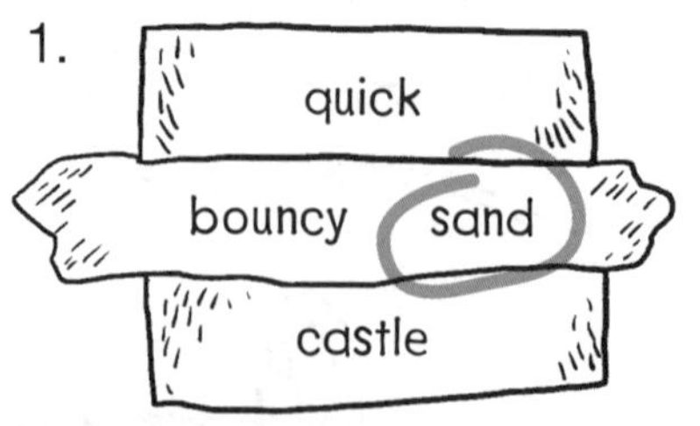

2.
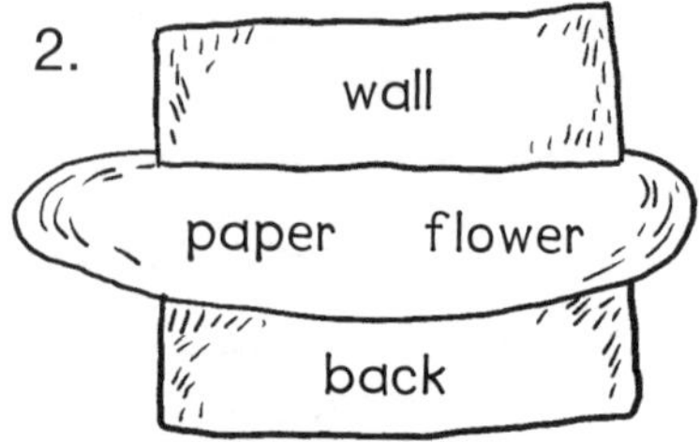

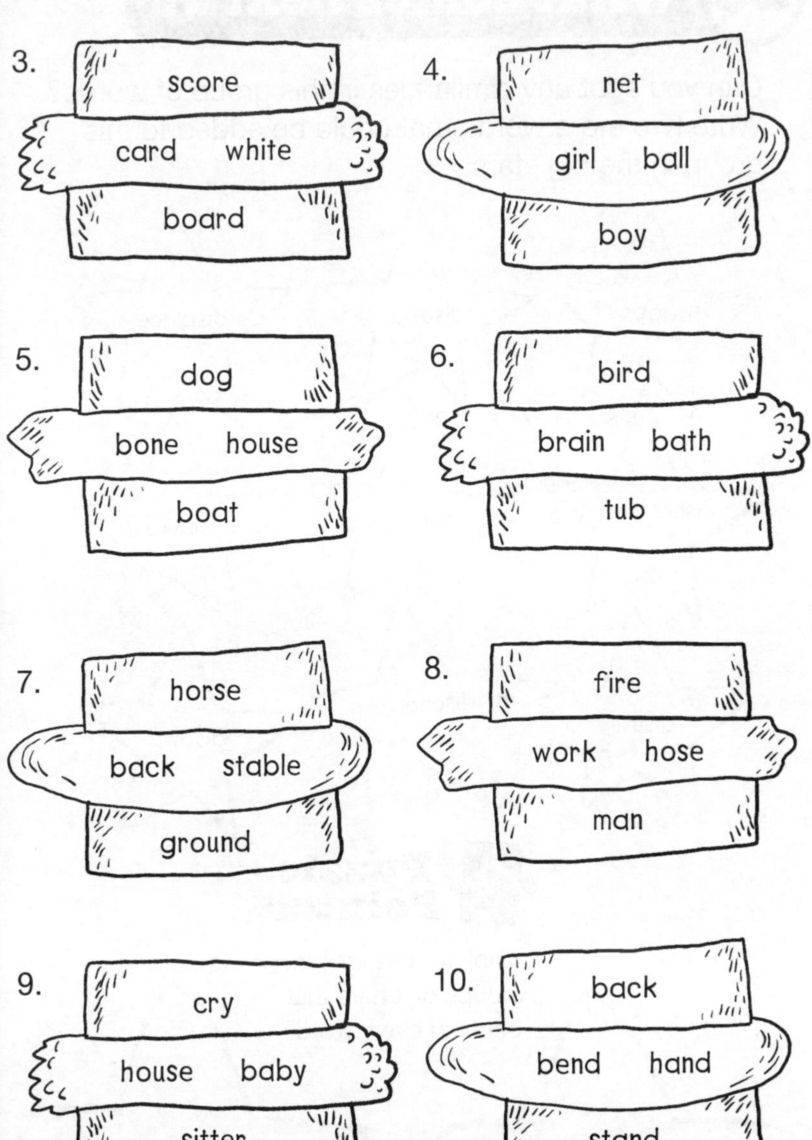
3.
score
card white
board
4.
net
girl ball
boy
5.
dog
bone house
boat
6.
bird
brain bath
tub
7.
horse
back stable
ground
8.
fire
work hose
man
9.
cry
house baby
sitter
10.
back
bend hand
stand

29 What comes next 1?

Can you spot any similarities in this group of words? Write two more words that could be added to this group in the big stars.

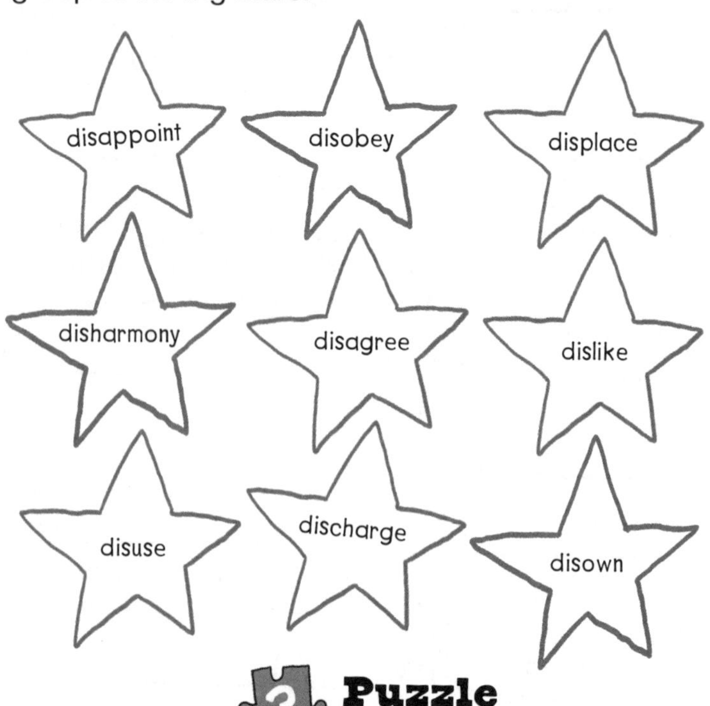

Puzzle Pointer

Look for patterns in groups of letters that occur in every word.

30 Rhymes and climbs

How quickly can you climb these word ladders? To answer each clue look at the previous word in the word ladder and change one letter to find a word that rhymes.

5. A sudden, quick movement, especially of the fingers. — 5. ______
4. Something done smoothly and impressively. — 4. ______
3. A short, sharp sound. — 3. ______
2. A painful, stiff feeling in the neck. — 2. ______
1. A cunning act. — 1. trick

Start Here ↑ thick

10. Thick rubber or plastic tube containing electrical wires. — 10. ______
9. Furniture you can eat on. — 9. ______
8. Black colour; an animal hunted for its fur. — 8. ______
7. Triangular end of a roof; Anne of Green _ _ _ _ _ s — 7. ______
6. A short story with a moral; Aesop's _ _ _ _ _ s — 6. fable

Start Here ↑ Mable

Puzzle Pointer

If you're not sure about a clue, go on to the next one, and then go back to it.

31 Spell it out!

Warm-up

Mr Brown has given Daisy some mnemonics to help her to remember her spellings. Using the clues, can you write the correct spellings for Daisy in the table? The first one has been done for you.

Daisy's misspelt word	Mr Brown's mnemonic clues	Correct spelling
1. bisness	Go to work on a **bus**.	business
2. calender	**C**heetahs **a**nd **l**ions **e**njoy **n**ightly **d**ances **a**fter **r**oaring.	
3. iland	**I s**leep on the **land**.	
4. noledge	**K**itty **n**ips **o**ver the **w**all and **l**icks **E**wan's **d**og, **G**eorgie **E**vans.	
5. freind	**I** before **e,** except after **c**.	
6. ocassional	I sometimes feed **two c**ats and **one s**nake.	
7. potatos	The pot ... tickles my **toes**.	
8. seperate	An **a**lligator splits things in two.	

Notepad

Make up your own mnemonic for the word **mnemonic**!

32 Word wall 2

Nine pairs of bricks on this wall are antonyms. Two bricks don't have an opposite and are the odd ones out. Circle and join all the matching pairs. Which two bricks are left over? Can you write an antonym for each of them?

villain	quiet	public	furthest
create	descend	sharp	wealth
private	freeze	hero	bold
blunt	last	cautious	boil
ascend	noisy	destroy	poverty

The odd words out are: ____________________ ____________________

Their antonyms are: ____________________ ____________________

Puzzle Pointer

An antonym is a word that has an opposite meaning to another word. For example, **larger** is the opposite and an antonym of **smaller**. Words can have more than one antonym. **Bigger** is another antonym of **smaller**.

33 The Daily Giggle

Read the newspaper review of a performance by stand-up comic, Badeea Badour. Find and circle the 12 **funny** words in the review that tell the reader it's about comedy.

Don't forget to check the review title and newspaper name when you're looking for the words.

The Daily Giggle

A fun night out

Stand-up comic Badeea Badour performed in front of a sell-out crowd at The Big Arena last Saturday. She had the crowd in the palm of her hand with her hilarious opening joke about supermarket self-service checkouts. Her witty and playful exchanges with members of the audience had even the most solemn people cracking a laugh.

The improvisation section of Badeea's act was particularly amusing, with the audience shouting out random, humorous topics for her to act out. The whole evening was a jovial night out and everyone left feeling cheerful.

The 12 funny words you circled in *The Daily Giggle* appear in the word search below. Find them and circle each one. They are written forwards, backwards, up, down or diagonally.

b e j j c ☺ a l u c
s c o m i c a ☺ ☺ h
☺ k v e ☺ u m s t e
e h i e g ☺ u n y e
y u a h ☺ o s s u r
t e l h r o i ☺ n f
t e y o ☺ c n o m u
i b m e l g g i g l
w u s l u f y a l p
h i l a r i o u s ☺

The leftover letters written in order spell out the answer to this side-splitting joke.

Why do bees have sticky hair?

_ _ _ _ _ _ _ _ _ _ _

_ _ _ _ _ _ _ _ _ _ _ _ _ !

34 The slipper thief

How observant are you? Would you make a good police officer? Can you spot and circle the **11 adjectives** in Officer Pickle's report about a robbery at a shoe shop? Fit the adjectives you have found into the correct places in the crossword grid opposite.

At two o'clock yesterday afternoon, my colleague and I arrived at the scene of the robbery. I ordered the staff to close the shop, and we commenced the mammoth task of searching for evidence. I found exhibit A: a triangular tag from a large dog's collar with the name Muncher on it.

I soon met the owner of this collar, and the thief, too. Behind the counter, next to a monumental pile of slippers, and with a slipper in his mouth, was Muncher. I was nervous and my mouth was dry, but my stalwart colleague helped me to coax Muncher away from the slippers. We didn't have to worry as Muncher was tame, although he looked rather thin.

We would like to thank the staff for their tremendous help. We are looking for Muncher's owners, but for now he is at the police station tucking into a mountainous bowl of food.

Puzzle Pointer

You are only looking for describing words, for example **stalwart** means **brave** and **reliable**, and describes Officer Pickle's colleague.

Write the correct letters in the boxes below to spell out the answer to the joke.

What do you do if your dog chews a dictionary?

F2	F10		C6
		K	

A6	G2	H11

G9	E2	F11	G6	A12

A3	D5	D9

A10	
	F

G2	F4	C9

H10	H6	A11	H8	J10

!

35 Word pyramid 1

These sand rats are curious! Write the answers to the clues in the pyramid. All the answers contain the word **rat**.

Clues

1. Rodent with a long tail and pointed snout.
2. Expression of annoyance or irritation.
3. Relationship between two amounts, for example 3:1.
4. Japanese fighting sport.
5. Work a machine; or what surgeons do to patients in a hospital.
6. Thankful for something.
7. P.E. equipment.
8. Place where science experiments are done.

36 Crossword challenge 1

Warm-up

Homophones sound the same, but have different meanings and can have different spellings. Can you guess the homophone for each of the words? Write your answers in the crossword grid.

■	■	■	1					■	■
2				■	■	■	■	3	■
	■	■		■	■	4 s	o	n	■
	■	5					■		■
	■	■		■	■		■		■
■	6			■	■		■		■
■		■	■	■	7		8		
■		■	■	9	■	■		■	■
■	10				■	■		■	■
■		■	■		■	■	■	■	■

Across clues
1. plane
2. ball
4. sun
5. site
6. by
7. great
10. not

Down clues
1. place
2. banned
3. night
4. stare
6. break
8. ad
9. eight

Puzzle Pointer

Some words may have more than one homophone. The challenge is to select the correct one that fits in the crossword.

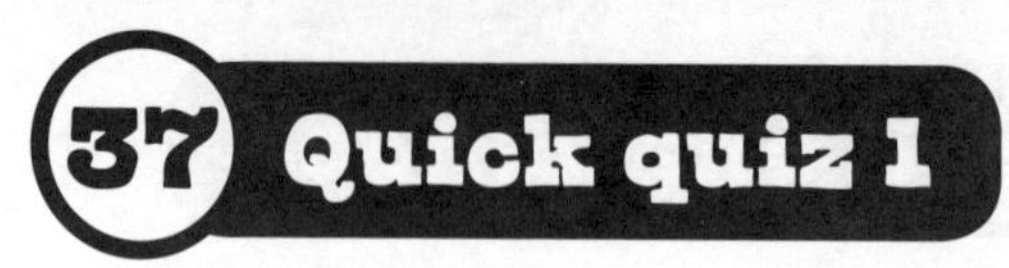

37 Quick quiz 1

Warm-up

How much do you remember from the warm-up puzzles and how much of a quiz-whizz are you? Circle the letter next to the correct answer to each of these questions. Then write the letters beside your answers in the answer boxes, in order, to spell out the rather strange nickname of a bird.

1. This **ch** word completes the expression: Don't count your __________ before they hatch.

   H children **B** chickens

2. This **que** word is always older than you.

   A macaque **U** antique

3. You will spot this creature in the rainforest.

   T chameleon **P** polar bear

4. What is a **homophone** for **great**?

   E grayt **T** grate

5. Add this word to **over** to make a new word.

   R zero **E** come

6. This word means the same as **tiny**.

   K tremendous **R** microscopic

7. This letter is the fourth vowel in the alphabet.

B O **N** I

8. Using the mnemonic I sleep on the land, which is the correct spelling for a desert **iland**?

U island **A** eyeland

9. Which word is an **antonym** of **villain**?

T criminal **M** hero

10. This word can be made from some of the letters in the word **chameleon**.

E lime **P** lemon

The bird is a

.

Warm-up

Puzzle power!

How did you do? Do you have puzzle power? Check the answers at the end of the book and add up how many warm-up puzzles you got right. Score 2 for each fully correct puzzle, and 1 if you got some of the puzzle right. Then write down your total and read on to discover your puzzle power...

My puzzle power score is ______ **.**

Puzzle power score 1–25

It can take a little while to warm up your puzzle power. Why don't you go over some of the puzzles you weren't sure about before going on to the next puzzles?

Puzzle power score 26–49

Well done. Your puzzle power is growing and you're getting warmed up for the intermediate puzzles. Maybe you can grab a dictionary to help you on your next puzzle quest.

Puzzle power score 50+

Wow, you have dazzling puzzle power! You are ready to zoom straight to the intermediate puzzles and take on some more puzzle challenges.

Intermediate puzzles

38 Riddle time!

Find the letters that appear more than six times in box 1, and more than four times in box 2. Then unscramble the letters to spell out the answer to the joke. Write the answer in the boxes.

What is as big as an elephant but weighs nothing?

Intermediate

39 Pick up sticks

Write the letter from each stick, starting with the stick on the top of the pile, to spell out the answer to the joke below.

What do you get if you cross a cocker spaniel, a poodle and a rooster?

A ______________________________ !

Intermediate

40 Guess the letter 1

ABCDEFGHIJKLMNOPQRSTUVWXYZ

Starting with the letter in the star, follow the instructions and guess which letter you end up at in the alphabet. Write the letter in the empty star at the bottom of the page.

f

Instructions

1. Go forwards five letters.
2. Advance to the next vowel.
3. Go back the number of letters in the missing word in this sentence: Humpty Dumpty is a character in a nursery __________ .

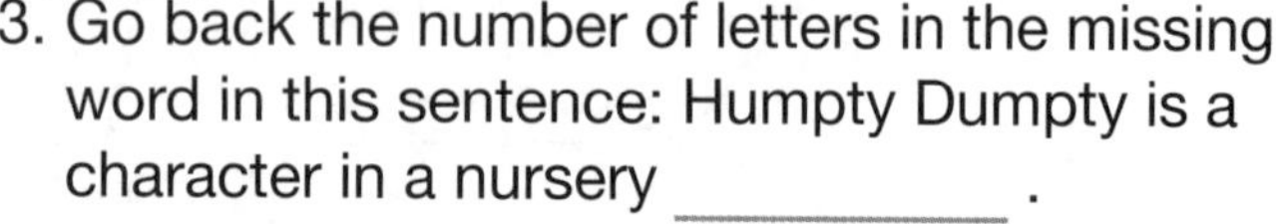

4. Jump backwards the number of vowels in the alphabet.
5. Slide forwards the number of consonants in the alphabet.
6. Retreat 20 steps.

Puzzle Pointer

Use the alphabet at the top of the page to help you as you follow the instructions.

41 Picture puzzle 2

Look at the pictures and follow the instructions to delete and add letters. Can you spell out the joke?

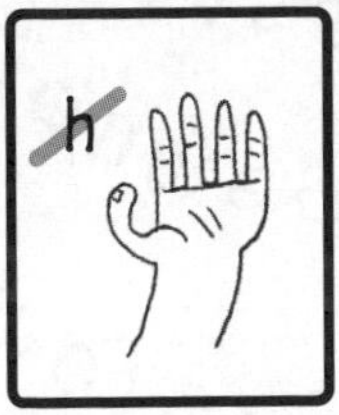

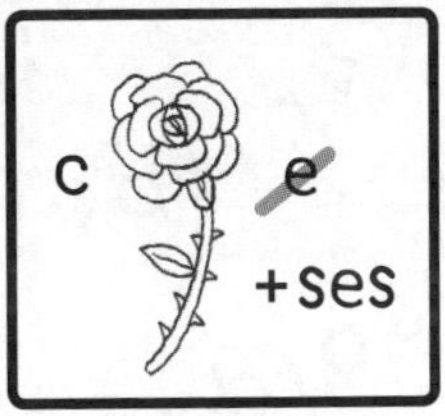

~~le~~ +t

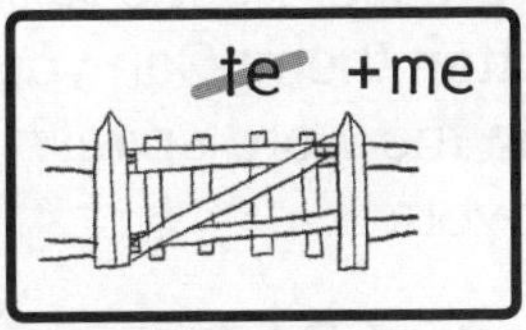

~~te~~ +me

~~or~~

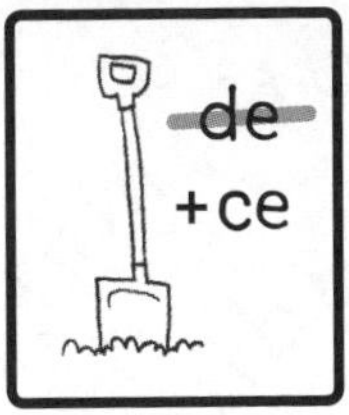

~~de~~ +ce

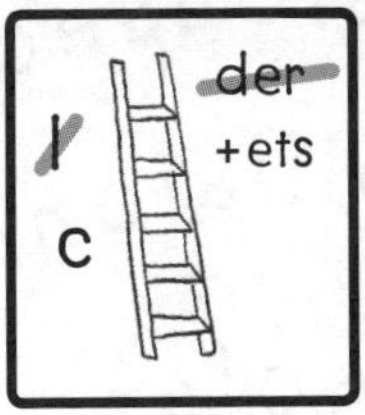

~~l~~ c ~~der~~ +ets

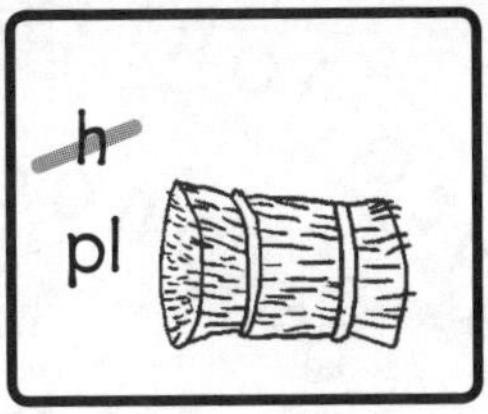

~~h~~ pl ?

a+ ~~aw~~ + on+ ~~umn~~ +s

~~h~~

c ~~e~~ +ses !

What ____ __ _____
_____ ____?
____
___ _______!

Intermediate

42 Mention the invention!

Professor Rhinepine has invented a crazy potion. It can be used for things that **contain** the letters **tion**, in order. The professor needs to list all these things, but she's forgotten them! Can you help her by circling the ten things in the word spiral? The first one has been found for you.

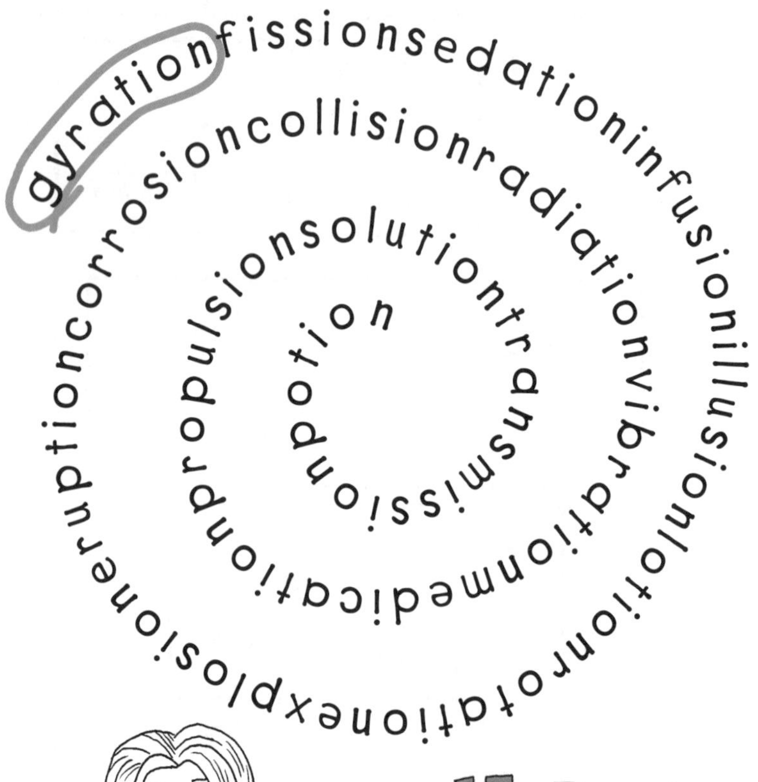

Intermediate

gyrationfissionsedationinfusionillusionlotionrotationexplosioneruptioncorrosioncollisionradiationvibrationmedicationpropulsionsolutiontransmissionpotion

Remember, the words need to contain the four letters **tion** in order, and not **sion**!

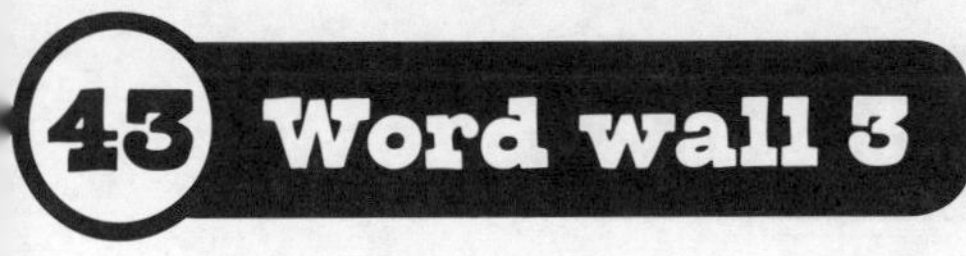

43 Word wall 3

Can you spot a theme to the words in this wall?

gallant
distant
consultant
tyrant
radiant

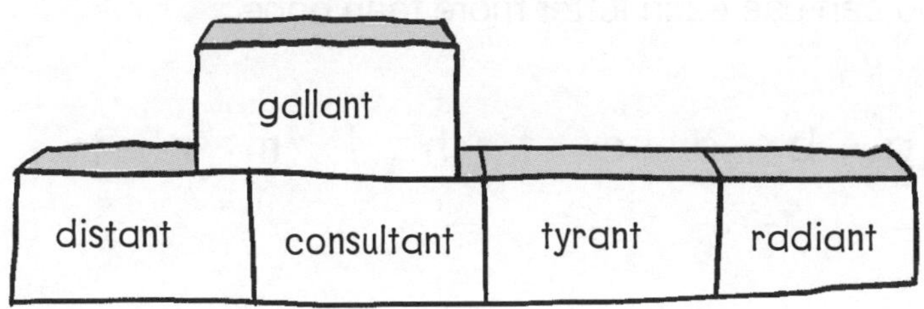

Not all the bricks from the pile below can be used in the wall because they don't follow the same theme. Shade the bricks in the pile that can be used.

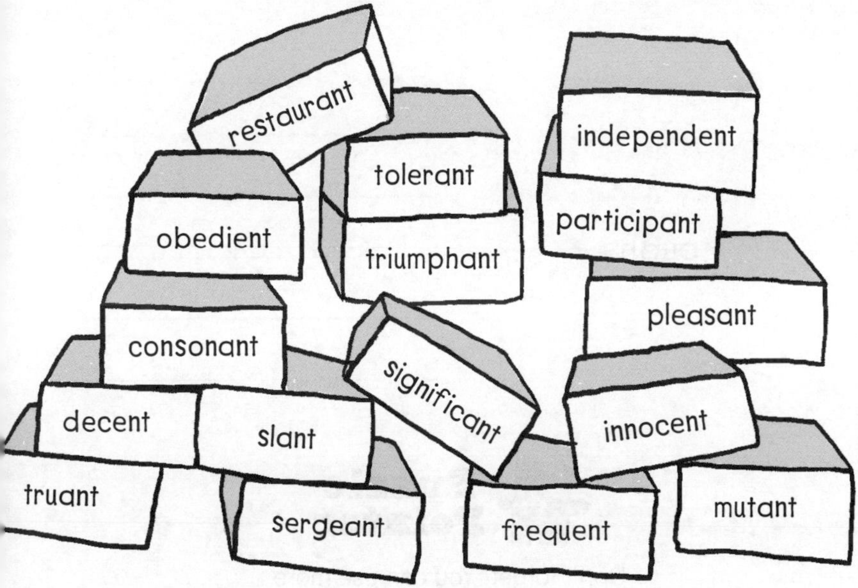

restaurant
tolerant
independent
obedient
participant
triumphant
pleasant
consonant
significant
decent
slant
innocent
truant
sergeant
frequent
mutant

Add one or more of the letters below in front of the letters in the circles to create five words for each. You can use each letter more than once.

a b c e f h l n r t

Intermediate

ought

ough

Don't forget! You can use more than one additional letter.

45 Pick up swords

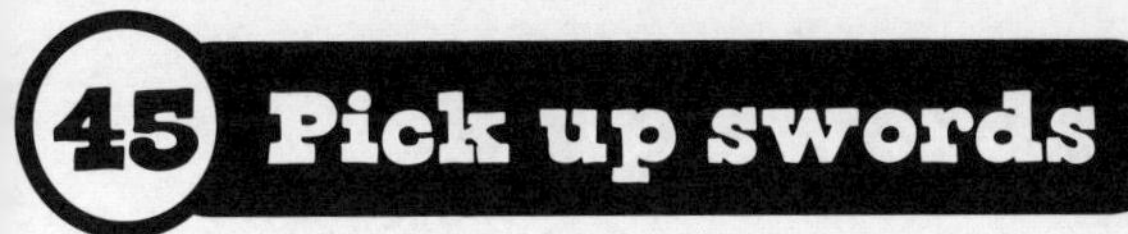

Write the letter from each sword, starting with the sword on the top of the pile, to spell out the answer to the joke below.

Who invented King Arthur's round table?

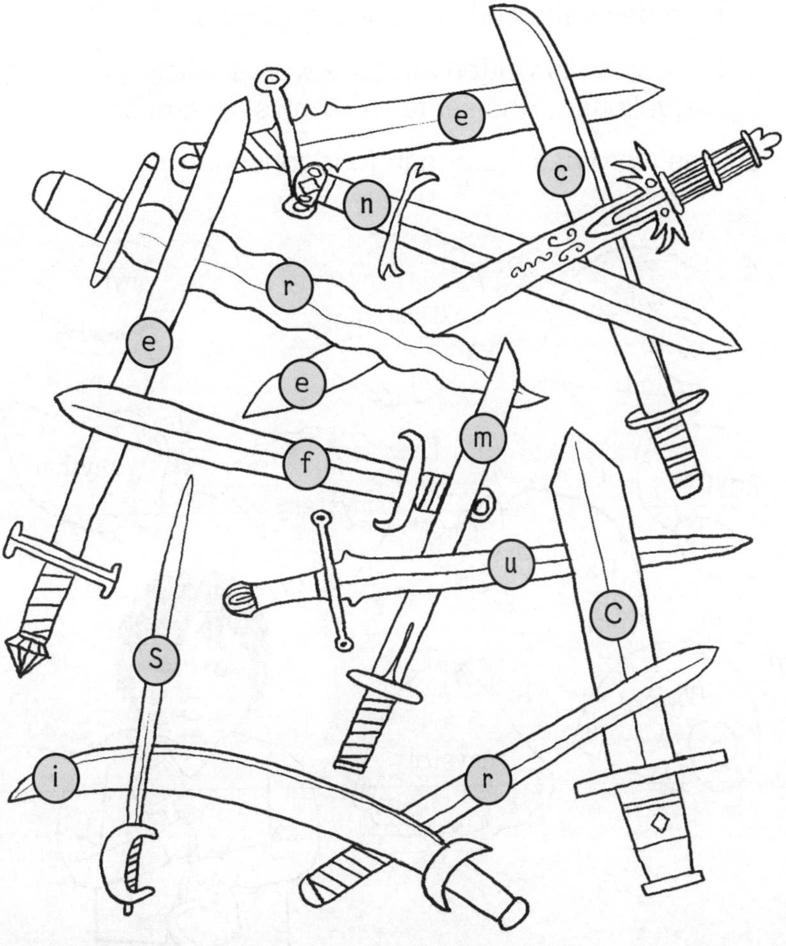

Intermediate

46 Guess the word 1

Read the clues and guess the word. This word is written on the shell that Akio wants to add to his collection. Circle the shell with the correct word.

Clues

1. It contains only one vowel.
2. It doesn't start with a letter that's before H in the alphabet.
3. It contains the 20th letter in the alphabet.
4. If the word is written after the words 'Mickey's marvellous…' the sentence shows alliteration.
5. This word has more than four consonants.

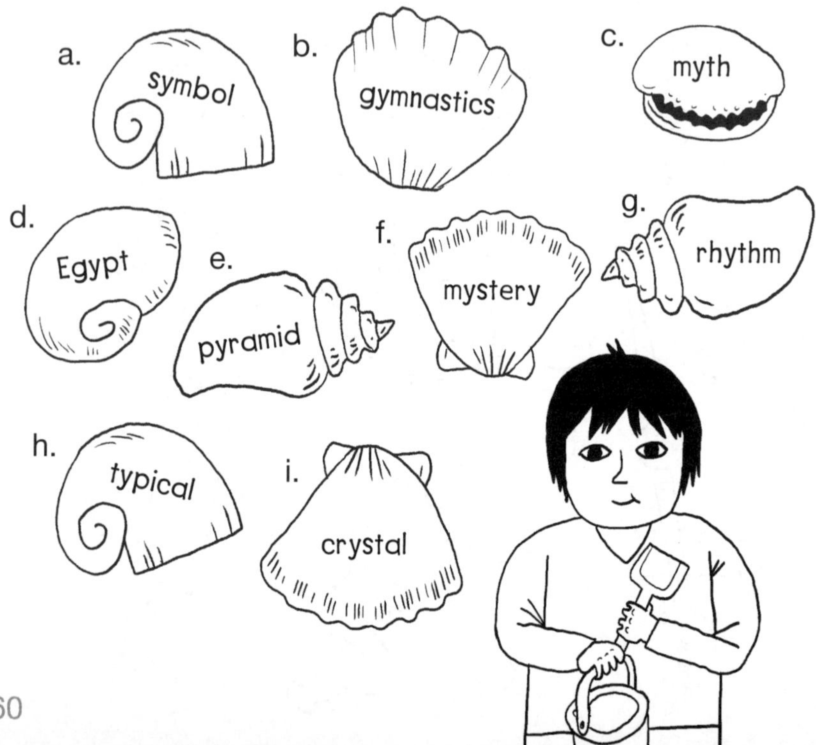

Intermediate

47 Word sandwiches 2

Can you circle the correct word filling for each sandwich? The filling must make a new word when added to the end of the top word, and it must make a different new word when added to the beginning of the bottom word. The first one has been done for you.

1. tomb
brick stone
wall

2. cart
wheel horse
barrow

3. fire
wood hose
land

4. eye
sore sight
see

5. wind
screen time
play

6. cat
jump walk
about

7. mouth
wash sore
basin

8. whole
meal lunch
time

9. water
fall can
out

10. ball
ship room
mate

Intermediate

48 Puzzle muddle

Can you help Fergus solve his puzzle muddle? The words in each group have the same meaning, except for one word, which is the odd one out. Write this word on the answer line. Then write the answers, in order, in the word spiral. Finally, unscramble the shaded letters to spell out how Fergus feels.

Intermediate

end – finish – start – complete ______ start

timid – courageous – brave – bold ______

miserable – happy – sad – glum ______

exciting – mundane – dull – tiresome ______

wander – walk – waddle – whizz ______

whispered – mumbled – yelled – muttered ______

gently – softly – delicately – harshly ______

firstly – finally – primarily – initially ______

Puzzle Pointer

Some words may be written backwards!

Answer _ r a _ _ _ _ _

49 Word pyramid 2

There is so much sand in the Sahara desert it's getting in everything, even these words! Write the answers to the clues in the pyramid. All the answers contain the word **sand**.

1. ☐☐☐☐
2. ☐☐☐☐☐
3. ☐☐☐☐☐☐
4. ☐☐☐☐☐☐☐
5. ☐☐☐☐☐☐☐☐
6. ☐☐☐☐☐☐☐☐☐
7. ☐☐☐☐☐☐☐☐☐☐

Clues

1. You'll find lots of this in a desert and on beaches.
2. Hair this colour is a light yellowish-brown.
3. Light shoe with a strap worn in hot weather.
4. Shallow box in the ground containing sand for children to play in.
5. Two slices of bread, with a layer of food in between.
6. Strong wind in the desert carrying sand through the air.
7. One of a 1000 equal parts of something.

Intermediate

50 Who done it?

A priceless diamond has been stolen! There is one eyewitness, but he is having trouble remembering what the suspect looks like.

First, find and cross off all the suspects' surnames in the word search. You will find them written forwards, backwards, up, down or diagonally.

Intermediate

Fitzwaddle Pipsquill MacIntosh

Gobbler Antwhistle Turnip

Crimpdash Dashwood

a	n	t	w	h	i	s	t	l	e
d	l	u	d	d	d	t	l	h	l
w	d	r	d	t	d	i	s	s	d
d	d	n	d	d	u	o	i	a	d
n	d	i	h	q	t	e	s	d	a
a	d	p	s	n	d	h	d	p	w
d	d	p	i	d	w	n	d	m	z
d	i	c	d	o	d	t	d	i	t
p	a	g	o	b	b	l	e	r	i
m	d	d	d	d	d	a	s	c	f

Then circle the letters that are left over and write them in the notepad below.

Now cross off all the letter 'd's, as these are decoy letters.

Finally, unscramble the letters that are left to spell out the full name of the thief and write it in the box below.

Notepad

Intermediate

51 Word square 2

How many words of **four or more** letters can you make using the letters in this word square? Every word you make **must** contain the letter **r**. Names and plurals don't count. Use your puzzle power to spot a nine-letter word that can be made with all the letters.

o	i	t
e	r	o
a	p	n

Puzzle Pointer

Look for common letter combinations of **r** with a **vowel** before or after it, such as **ir** or **ra**, and go through the rest of the letters to see if any will join with these letters to make a word.

pair

Puzzle Pointer

Here's a clue to the nine-letter word. A surgeon performs this in a hospital.

52 Knight school

Young knight Korben thought he'd get lots of sleep at knight school. He was wrong! Unscramble the letters to spell out eight loud words that are keeping knight Korben awake.

1. w l a b b__________!
2. t l t r a e r__________!
3. a l t c t e r c__________!
4. h g n i e n__________!
5. h e e c r s c s__________!
6. n a j l e g j__________!
7. k r c l e a c c__________!
8. k h w t a c thwack__________!

Intermediate

53 Best Bakes

Welcome to the final round of the Best Bakes baking competition. Unfortunately, the judges are not too keen on the taste of many of them! Crack the codes for each answer and work out what the judges have said about each cake. Which cake is the winner?

Each answer has a different code. Look for a pattern between the cake's number and the answer.

1. distasteful

distasteful

2. aduiesogiussatoibnrg

disgusting

Intermediate

3. omaghbeaockmsairrnodagebcllofe

___

4. vearustesseprofuwstgoornertathenstot

___

5. dartdeargeoonslghtoirswograde
hoquftiorwfsamkuswawl

___

6. kindeliubghocafghaoomkitweriu
hrrhyuspliowosazdemloswae

___

7. rudlslrinhdjuesnchryvijdneyoslokielsl
oiuntaloiknialopqwnayunjig

___

8. loiuynjsewoiunthasdeomvoyhuikmnc
swerjikksaqwedrisernoplnasaliwpg

___

The winning cake is ________________ **.**

54 Word ladder 1

How quickly can you climb down this word ladder to help Zane reach home? To answer each clue, look at the previous word in the word ladder and change one letter. The first clue has been done for you.

If you're not sure of one answer, go on to the next answer and work backwards.

Intermediate

1. A single sheet of glass in a window or door.
2. An evergreen tree with needle-shaped leaves.
3. Very high quality.
4. Discover something, often after a long search.
5. Tie tightly together.
6. Share a strong connection with someone.
7. A skeleton is made of this.
8. Past tense of the word do.
9. A round, onion-shaped roof.

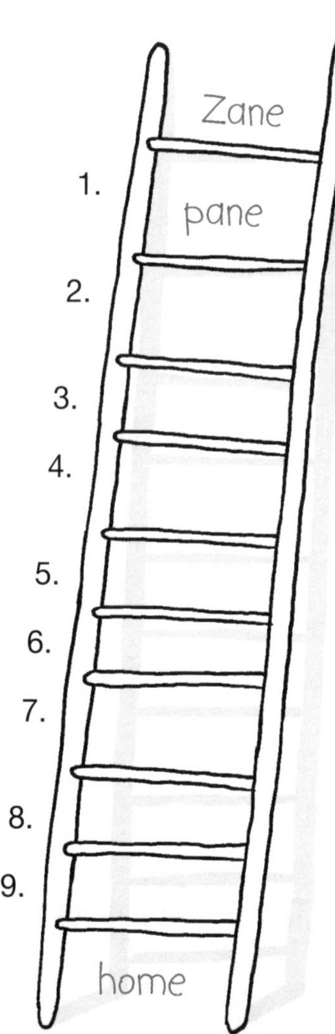

55 Guess the word 2

Read the clues and guess the password that will open the safe.

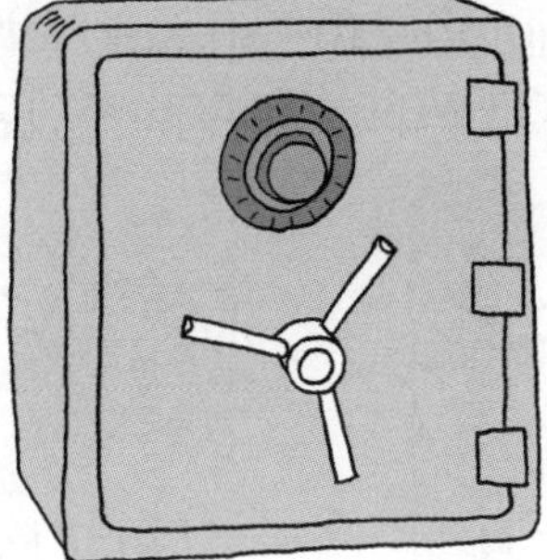

Clues

1. It has 7 letters.
2. It has the same two-letter suffix as matinee.
3. Some synonyms of the word are: judge, arbitrator, umpire, adjudicator, conciliator.
4. If it was the missing word in this sentence, the writer would be using alliteration.

   The ________________ ruthlessly reinforced the rules.
5. The word has the same number of syllables as the phrase, **can you see**.

The password is ________________ .

Notepad

Intermediate

56 Perfect Pooches

These are the winning dogs at Perfect Pooches dog show. Fit all their winning categories into the grid. Then unjumble the shaded letters in the shaded boxes and write the answer to the joke.

Place the word with the most letters in the grid first, and work your way down, ending with the word that contains the fewest letters.

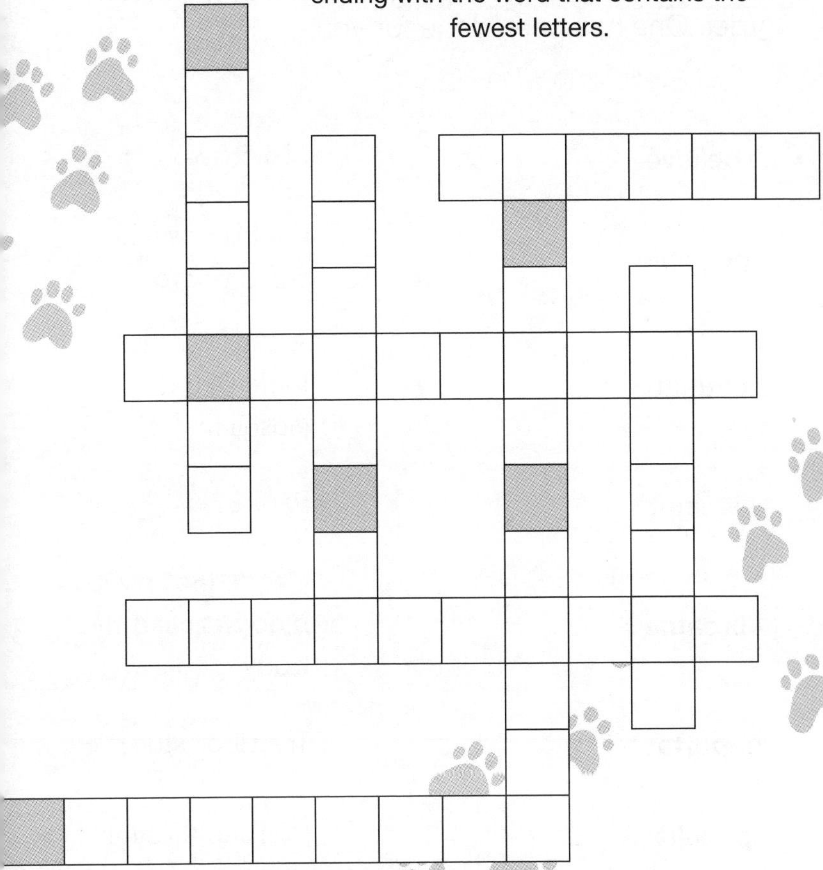

Intermediate

Why did one of the dogs at Perfect Pooches sweat so much?

Because he was a ___ ___ !

57 Find the words

Using some of the letters from each bold word on the left, can you make a shorter word that answers each clue? You may need to put the letters in a different order. One has been done for you.

Intermediate

Word	Answer	Clue
believe	☐☐☐☐	Stay alive.
possible	☐☐☐☐	Hold a position for a photo.
naughty	g n a t	A small fly that looks like a mosquito.
weight	☐☐☐☐☐	97 – 89 =
breathe	☐☐☐☐☐	Organ that pumps blood around the body.
important	t ☐☐☐☐	Tread or stamp on.
peculiar	c ☐☐☐☐	Can see through.
difficult	☐☐☐☐☐	Steep rock face near the sea.

58 Snow scare

Write the letter from each ski, starting with the ski on the top of the pile, to spell out what gave the children a fright on their recent school skiing trip.

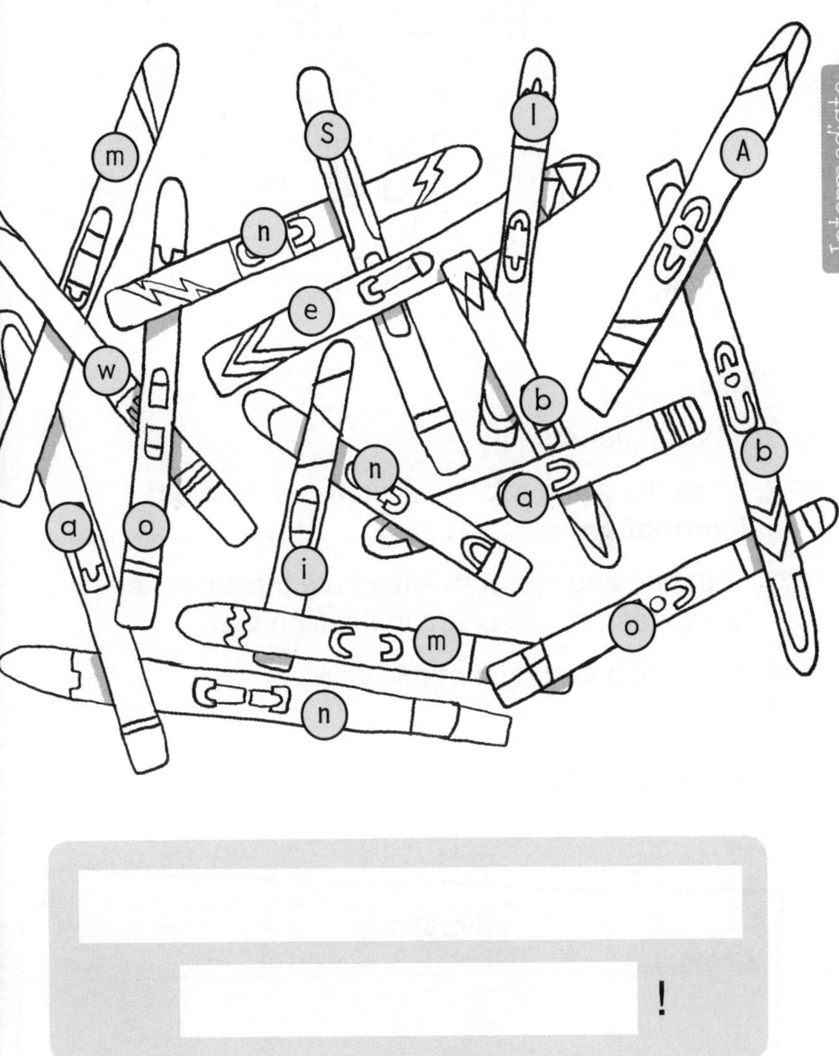

!

59 Guess the word 3

Read the clues and guess the password that will bring down the drawbridge.

Intermediate

Clues

1. It has 11 letters.
2. It has the same two-letter prefix as the word **information**.
3. The third and eleventh letters are the same as the sixteenth consonant in the alphabet.
4. Clever is a synonym of this word.

The password is ______________ .

Notepad

60 The bigger picture

Can you guess what common sayings these pictures show? Write your answers in the boxes.

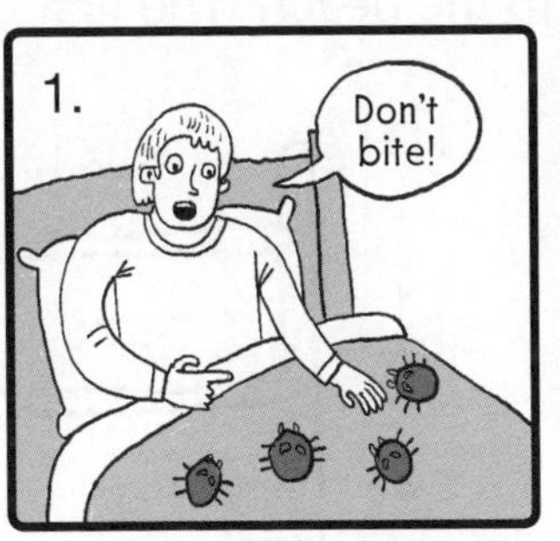

1. Don't ☐☐☐ ☐☐☐ ☐☐☐☐☐☐☐ ☐☐☐☐.

2. Let 

.

3. Two ☐☐☐☐☐ ☐☐☐ ☐☐☐☐☐☐ ☐☐☐☐ ☐☐☐.

4. It's ☐☐☐☐☐☐☐ ☐☐☐☐ ☐☐☐ ☐☐☐☐.

61 Word ladder 2

Change one letter at a time and rearrange the the new selection of five letters to answer the clues and help Bilal go from the hotel to the beach. The first clue has been done for you.

Intermediate

1. Took something that doesn't belong to you.
2. The smallest amount.
3. A very strong metal.
4. A small sugar snack.
5. To perspire after exercise.
6. A crop grown in fields, ground to make flour.

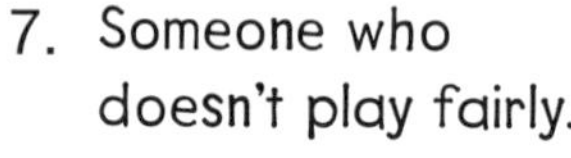

7. Someone who doesn't play fairly.

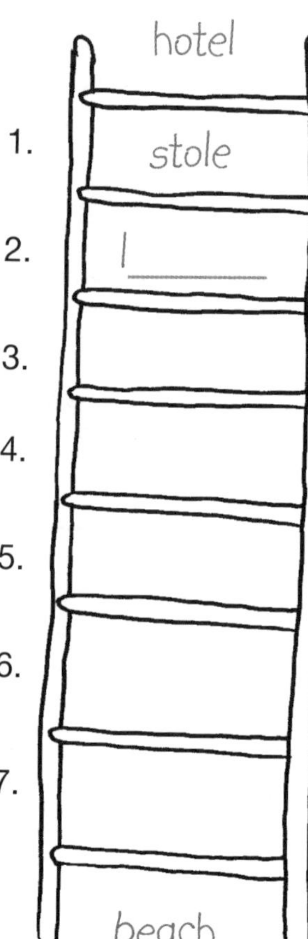

62 Picture this 2

Can you guess the words shown in these illustrations? Unscramble the letters in each root word and choose the correct word ending from below to make each word.

Now draw your own illustration of a word with one of these endings. Muddle the letters of its root word and see if a friend can guess the word.

63 Mischief-makers

These troublesome pupils are in detention. Can you fit their misdemeanours and the problems they have caused into the grid? Unscramble the letters in the shaded boxes and write them in the answer box to complete the joke.

Place the word with the most letters in the grid first, and work your way down, ending with the word that contains the fewest letters.

- mischief
- misconduct
- mishap
- missing
- miscount
- mischievous
- mistime
- miserable

Why did the burglar rob a bakery?

Because he needed the !

Intermediate

64 Password puzzle

The bank manager of BLUFF bank has forgotten the password to the safe again. Using some of the letters from each bold word on the left, can you make a shorter word to answer each clue? Then write the first letter of each answer, in order, in the answer boxes. Shout out the word, and hey presto, open the safe!

Intermediate

forward	☐☐☐☐	A single unit in a sentence.
perhaps	☐☐☐☐	Listen to.
position	☐☐☐☐	Expression when you've made a mistake.
opposite	o p p o s e	Disagree with.
disappear	☐☐☐☐☐	You have this when you are pleased with your achievements.
breath	☐☐☐☐☐	The planet we live on.
separate	☐☐☐☐	Compass point opposite west.

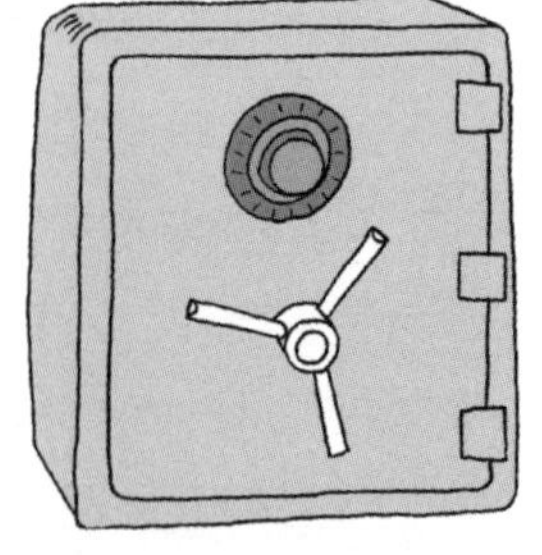

☐☐☐ o ☐☐☐ !

65 Roaring names

Unscramble the names of seven dinosaurs. Can you guess which name belongs to the dinosaur in the illustration? Its name means **spiny lizard** as it had a huge spiny sail on its back and was the biggest meat-eating dinosaur that ever lived!

The names share three different word endings. Look for patterns and work out the word ending first.

1. urnunaTyroass xeR ______________________
2. cirVeloaport ______________________
3. rausogStesu ______________________
4. otarTriceps ______________________
5. suroSpinaus ______________________
6. iosBrachurusa ______________________
7. Protopcerotas ______________________

Intermediate

66 Diary of a knight

Read the diary extract below and use the list of words to fill in the missing gaps. Some words may fit in more than one space, so choose which one makes the most sense. You must fill every gap and no word can be used more than once.

anxious	furious	glacial	hurtled
proficient	humongous	heroic	horrendous
massive	watery	incredibly	sweet
exciting	official	brilliantly	

Intermediate

Don't forget that **an** is used before words that start with a vowel.

My name is Lance Moat and I live with my family in an ________________ grand castle, and I'm training to be a ________________ knight.

Read my diary to see what ________________ things I got up to yesterday...

Monday 6 January 1405

Morning

The day didn't start ________________ as I slept in this cold, ________________ morning so didn't have time for breakfast. Instead I swiped some

__________ chunks of bread and cheese from the table as I __________ past, as fast as a galloping horse.

I was late for my arithmetic lesson and was __________ Mr Bodmass would be __________ with me. But it wasn't so __________, as I managed to sneak in at the back, so I don't think Mr Bodmass noticed I was late.

Afternoon

There was just time for a brisk lunch of pottage (that's __________ vegetable soup to you twenty-first century readers!) and a mug of __________ milk after my morning lessons. Then I spent the afternoon on horseback doing my favourite thing in the world: riding a horse at full speed, holding a __________ lance and trying to spear rings on the tip of the lance. I'm practising with a blunt lance, but when I get older and become more __________ at it, I'll get to use an __________ sharp lance.

Intermediate

67 Backwards and forwards

All the answers to these clues read the same backwards as they do forwards. Answer each clue, then write the letters in the shaded boxes, in order, in the answer boxes to spell out the name of this type of word. One clue has been done for you.

Intermediate

Look quickly and secretively.

Type of canoe.

Performances given alone.

Connected to a city or a town. c i v i c

Girl's name. H

System to show aircraft in the sky. r a

Type of blade on a helicopter. t

Expression of surprise. w

A polite shopkeeper may call a woman this. "Can I help you, __ __ d __ __ ?" d

A flat and even surface.

A

is the name given to a word that reads the same backwards as forwards.

68 Word ladder 3

Change one letter at a time and rearrange the new selection of five letters to answer the clues and get to Ewan's holiday destination. Where is Ewan going on holiday?

1. Flavour of food or drink in your mouth.
2. Make _ _ _ _ _ ; speed up or hurry.
3. Instruct someone; help them learn.
4. Not expensive.
5. Run after something to catch it.
6. Bash into something.
7. Something to sit on.
8. Destination (its capital is Beijing).

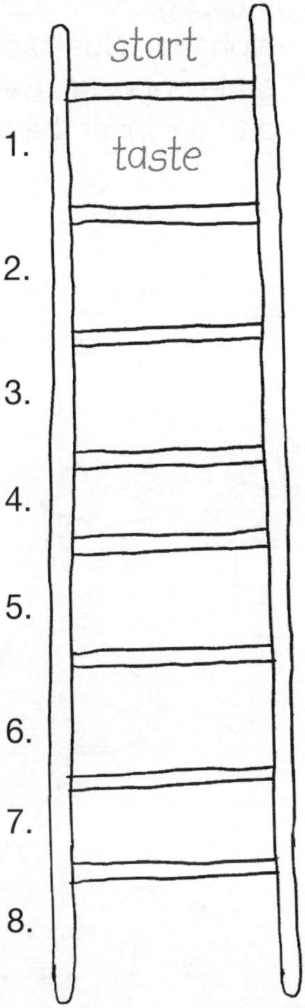

start

1. taste

2.

3.

4.

5.

6.

7.

8.

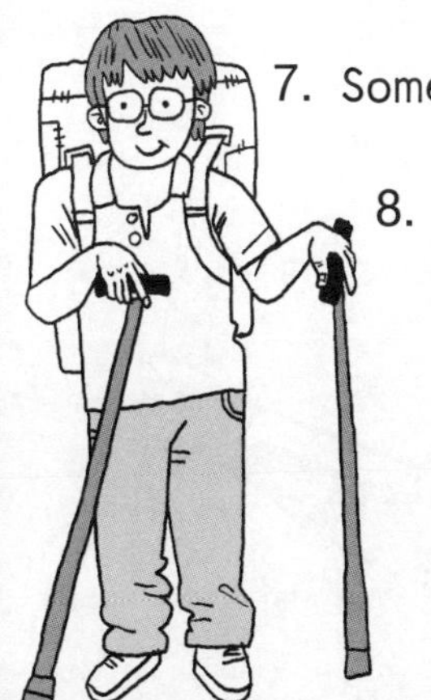

Intermediate

69 Cave code

Intrepid explorer Noe (short for Norah) Zee Parker has travelled back in time to 10 000 BCE and found these Stone Age cave paintings. The pictures are a coded message, with each animal standing for a letter of the alphabet. Noe has filled in some of the letters in the table opposite. Can you work out the rest of the letters and decipher the answer to the joke?

If you don't know every creature, try working out the answer with the letters you do know.

			ostrich		iguana	
			s		g	

Do you notice a pattern between the animal names and the letters Noe has filled in? Write the names of the other creatures underneath their pictures. Then crack the code and fill in the rest of the letters.

Write the letters in order in the answer boxes below to spell out the answer to the joke.

Teacher: What came after the Stone Age?

Pupil: !

70 Hunt the homophones

Guess the homophone for each of these words. Then find and cross off your answers in the word search. You will find them written forwards, backwards, up, down or diagonally.

currant current
mist ____________
read ____________
weather ____________
heal ____________
rein ____________
sent ____________
wear ____________
groan ____________
mousse ____________
seen ____________

wail ____________
meddle ____________
rays ____________
serial ____________
wood ____________

Look for words in the word search, and then see if they are homophones to any of the words.

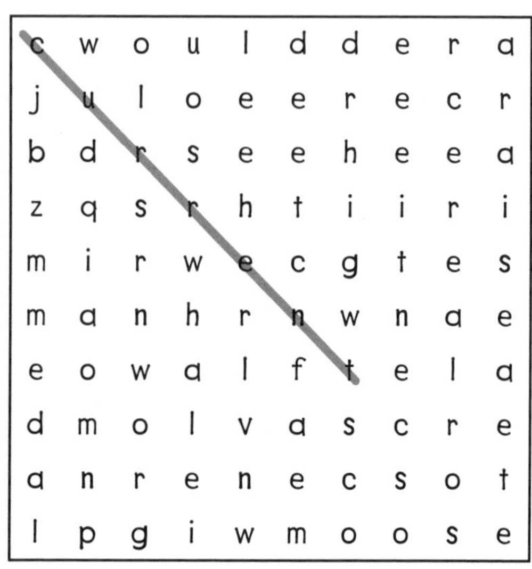

71 Antonym antics

How well do you know your antonyms? Write the antonym opposite each word. Then write the answers in order, into the word spiral. Finally, unscramble the shaded letters to spell out the answer to the joke.

question __________

natural artificial

despair __________

vertical __________

obedient __________

youngest __________

compulsory __________

The antonyms are in alphabetical order.

Intermediate

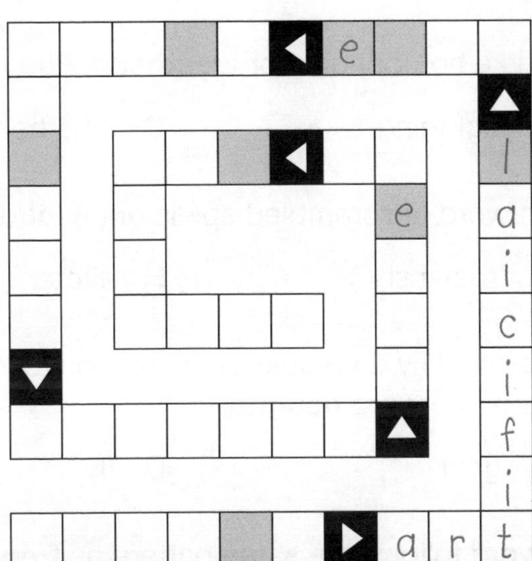

What starts with e, ends with e, and only has one letter?

An  e _ _ _ l _ _ e  !

72 Quick quiz 2

It's time to test how much you remember from the intermediate puzzles. Circle the letter next to the correct answer to each of these questions. Then write the letters beside your answers in the answer boxes, in order. They will spell out the name of a creature with some amazing talents.

1. Which word is an antonym of **voluntary**?

   A compulsory **P** optional

2. This word is a synonym of **firstly**.

   A finally **R** primarily

3. What is a homophone for **weather**?

   R lightning **C** whether

4. Which word unscrambled spells out a **loud** word?

   R rpewhsi **H** altcter

5. Find a small fly that looks like a mosquito in the letters of the word **naughty**.

   E gnat **O** fly

6. This word follows the same pattern as **frequent** and **independent**.

   T triumphant **R** obedient

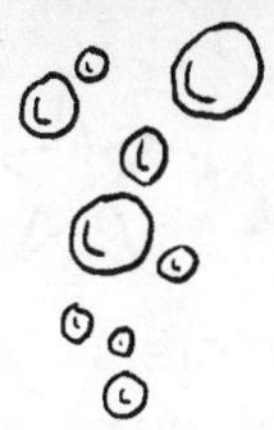

7. Which is this coded word **eduidsogpuosatmibnqgo**?

   B adventurous   **F** disgusting

8. This word is the opposite of **uneven** and reads the same forwards as backwards.

   E pump   **I** level

9. This word can be made from some of these letters: **i, r, o, o, e, p, t, a, n**.

   S parent   **A** present

10. This word means the same as the words **courageous** and **brave**.

   R timid   **H** bold

The underwater creature is an

☐☐☐☐☐☐☐☐☐☐.

Intermediate

Puzzle power!

Is your puzzle power building as you do more puzzles? Check the answers at the end of the book and add up how many intermediate puzzles you got right. Score 2 for each fully correct puzzle, and 1 if you got some of the puzzle right. Then write down your total and read on to discover your puzzle power...

My puzzle power score is  .

Puzzle power score 1–25

You like to take your time with things and have just dipped your toe in the puzzles. Look back over some of the puzzles before diving into the next ones.

Puzzle power score 26–49

You're splashing about and having fun with the puzzles. As your confidence grows, so does your puzzle power. Keep it up.

Puzzle power score 50+

You're zipping through with lightning speed and your puzzle power is electrifying. You are ready to take on some tricky puzzle challenges.

Tricky puzzles

73 What comes next 2?

Can you work out how all these verbs are similar? Write two more verbs that could be added to this group in the big stars.

Puzzle Pointer

Think about the type of sentence you would create with these words. There are a few other verbs you can choose.

Tricky

74 Guess the letter 2

ABCDEFGHIJKLMNOPQRSTUVWXYZ

Read the first instruction and write the letter you start at in the star at the top of the page. Then follow the rest and work out which letter you end up at. Write that letter in the star at the bottom of the page.

Puzzle Pointer

Use the alphabet at the top of the page to help you follow the instructions.

Tricky

Instructions

1. Start at the 12th consonant in the alphabet.
2. Advance eight letters.
3. Retreat the number of letters in the antonym of **smooth** that begins with an **r**.
4. Repeat clue 3.
5. Continue back to the next symmetrical letter.
6. Go forwards the number of vowels in the word that is a synonym of **zero**, begins with **n** and has six letters in total.

75 Moon munchies

These diners are eating at a fancy restaurant on the Moon, but their orders are muddled. Can you help clear up the mess and match each speech bubble to the person who said it? Add the correct numbers in the empty boxes next to each diner.

Tricky

1\. The fruit grown here on the Moon is the most environmentally friendly. Wouldn't you agree? But the vegetables are equally good.

2\. I'll have 500 millilitres of the tomato soup boiled to 100°C, and mixed with 100 grams of bread.

3\. Code seven. Salad. Over. Suspects include iceberg lettuce, tuna, cherry tomatoes, green beans and dressing. Confirm.

4\. Vanilla ice cream with raspberry sauce and cashew nuts please. I say, what did the nut say when it sneezed? Cashew!

5\. I'll give you ten team points if you give me olives for a starter. Did you know that an olive tree can live up to 600 years?

6\. Some succulent steak with crunchy hand-cut chips. Please can the chips be as crisp as autumnal leaves and the steak seasoned with a delicate hint of exotic pepper.

Tricky

76 Missing creatures 1

Read the clues for each group, and guess the name of a creature that can be added to the letters to make three words. The name of the creature can be added before, after or in the middle of the letters, but you cannot change the order of the letters.

Tricky

1.

Information and understanding.	knedge	Knowledge
Move around quietly.	pr	prowl
Any birds that people hunt.	wildf	wildfowl

2.

Hairy-skinned, small, green fruit.	berry	
Small bumps on the skin when the hairs are raised.	bumps	
Small mammal in Africa or Asia.	mon	

3.

Person or shop that sells this creature for food.	monger	
Sea creature with a clear soft body and tentacles.	jelly	
Not thinking of others.	sel	

4.

Tall plants with flowers shaped like the fingers of gloves.	glove	
Ballroom dance.	trot	
Beat someone by being more clever.	out	

77 Word sandwiches 3

Can you work out and write in the word filling for each sandwich? The filling must make a new word when added to the end of the top word, and it must make a different new word when added to the beginning of the bottom word. The first one has been done for you.

1. suit / case / book
2. country / ______ / show
3. stereo / t______ / writer
4. spot / ______ / house
5. un / ______ / quake
6. shell / f______ / tail
7. road / sh______ / case
8. road / ______ / line
9. sand / p______ / weight
10. under / s______ / by

Tricky

Puzzle Pointer

Start by thinking of words that can be added to the end of the top word to make a new word. Then try adding these words to the bottom word, one at a time, to see if you can make another new word.

78 Word square 3

How many words of **four or more** letters can you make using the letters in this word square? Every word you make **must** contain the letter **t**. Names and plurals don't count. Use your dazzling puzzle power to spot a nine-letter word that can be made with all the letters.

u	v	l
o	t	r
e	n	e

Here's a clue to the nine-letter word. You see lots of these helpful people at charity events.

Tricky

note

Look for common letter combinations, such as **te** or **ter**, and go through the rest of the letters to see if any will combine with these letters to make a word.

The biggest picture

How quickly can you guess what common sayings these pictures show? Write your answers in the boxes.

1.

2.

3.

4.

1. Have

2. Don't

Puzzle Pointer

Say exactly what you see in the picture.

3. A

4. A

Tricky

80 Odd one out 1

Can you guess the odd word out in each of these three groups of words? The first one has been done for you. Look for the same pattern in the two other groups.

Puzzle Pointer

Think about the type and function of words in each group.

Tricky

Read the clues and guess the word. This word is written on the shield that belongs to Sir Laughalot. Which one is the gallant knight's shield?

Tricky

Clues

1. Its initial letter is in the first third of the alphabet (about the first eight letters).
2. It contains more consonants than vowels.
3. Its second letter is in the second half of the alphabet.

Go through the clues in numerical order, and cross out the words it can't be.

82 Wacky weather

Each anagram on this weather map is the answer to a clue on the opposite page. Can you work out the words and write them in the correct places on the grid? The weather symbols will give you a clue.

Answer all the clues you can first, then go back to do the ones you're not sure of.

Tricky

hornsttmrdeu

bazzlird

dyolcu

tiglingnh

craneruih

matnisu

20°C

siuleCs

dorntoa

zizredl

bainwro

Clues

1. Cloud-covered sky.
2. Scale for measuring temperature. Shown as °C.
3. Light rain.
4. Arch of colours seen in the sky.
5. Violent winds in a funnel-shaped cloud.
6. Long, high wave caused by an earthquake.
7. Severe snowstorm.
8. Storm with a violent wind.
9. Electrical flash of light in a thunderstorm.
10. Storm with thunder, lightning and rain.

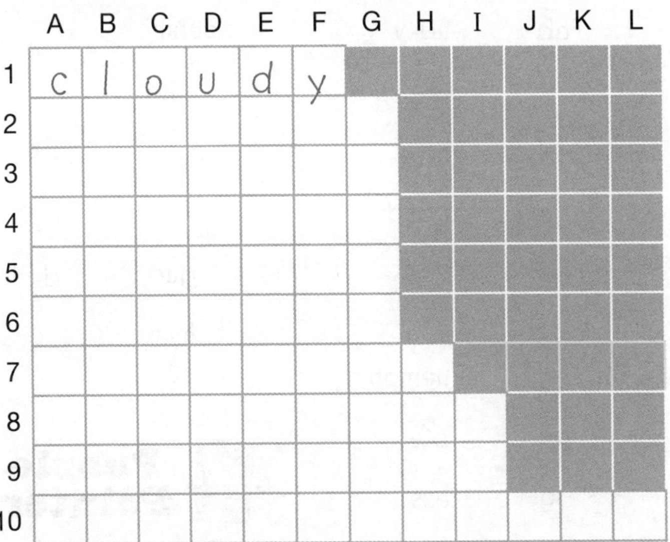

When you've filled in all the words, write the correct letters in the answer boxes to spell out the answer to this weather joke.

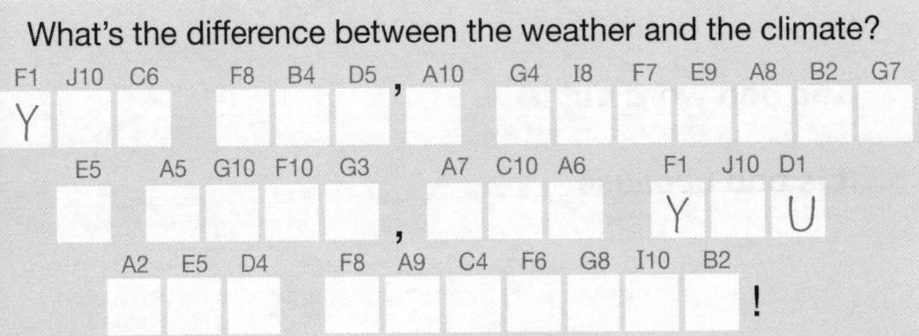

Tricky

83 Missing letters

Can you guess and write in the missing letter in these words? The missing letters in each word list will spell out three new words when read downwards. Which one of these words is the odd one out and why?

1.

han		some
Feb		uary
	a	isle
wei		h
le		pard
solem		

2.

g		itar
autum		
kn		t
s		issors
t		ugh
gua		d
hym		

3.

		nemonic
pe		ple
g		ess
i		land
lov		

Puzzle Pointer

Don't get caught out. Some of the missing letters may be silent letters!

The odd word out is ______________.

It is odd because ______________

______________.

Tricky

84 The Daily Rant

Choose the best words to fill in the gaps in *The Daily Rant* newspaper report below. A word can only be used once. But watch out as four of the words don't fit in the report!

abundant	elephants	hesitant	instant
arrogant	exuberant	ignorant	observant
elegant	giants	important	relevant

A few words can fit in each space. As long as the report makes sense, you can be creative with your word choices, using techniques such as alliteration.

You will never see such a beautiful sight as a herd of ________________ ________________ striding across the African savannah. It is ________________ to value these magnificent ________________ whose future is threatened by poaching and destruction of their habitat. And it's ________________ and ________________ to assume these ________________ beasts will live forever, as in an ________________ they may be gone.

Tricky

85 What comes next 3?

Can you work out how all these past tense words are similar? Write two more words that could be added to this group in the big stars.

Puzzle Pointer

How different is each verb to its present tense?

Tricky

86 Gift of the gab

Fill in the missing words to complete these expressions. Then write your answers in order into the word spiral. The last letter of each answer is the first letter of the next answer.

A bee in your bonnet.

A penny for your thoughts.

Head and ____________ above the rest.

Pull up your ____________.

He was found safe and ____________.

She was given the benefit of the ____________.

Barking up the wrong ____________.

He had ____________ on his face.

She heard it on the ____________.

They didn't see eye to ____________.

Tricky

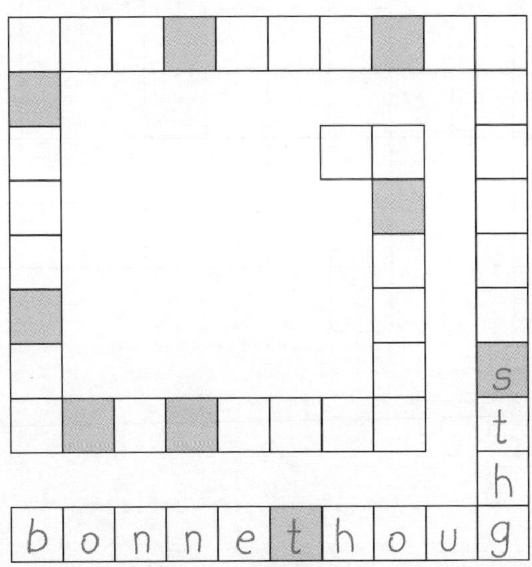

The words below agree with the mnemonic **i before e except after c**. Fit all the words into the grid, then unscramble the letters in the shaded boxes and write them in the answer boxes. They will spell out a word that is an exception to this rule.

ceiling	perceive
conceited	receipts
conceive	receive
deceit	receiver

s _ _ e _ _ _

Tricky

88 Word-eating machine

Professor Prime's machine needs words for fuel. Can you find 18 words of **4 or more** letters hidden inside the word ***experiment***? Write them in the boxes to feed the machine. Bigger words give the machine more power so the bigger the word, the better. But no plurals as the machine will spit these out!

Tricky

89 Odd one out 2

Can you guess the odd word out in each of these three groups of words? The first one has been done for you. Look for the same pattern in the two other groups.

1.

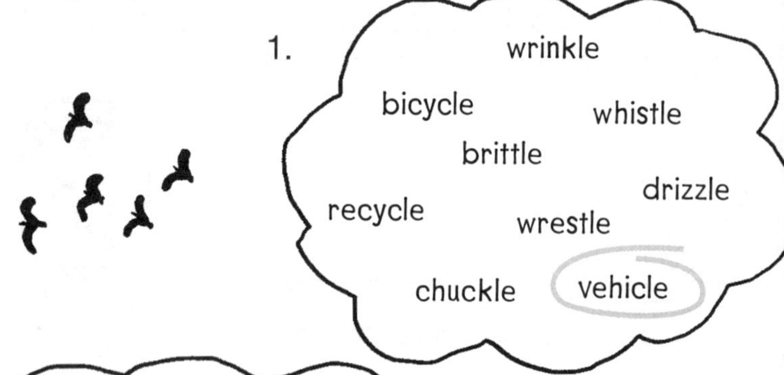

2.

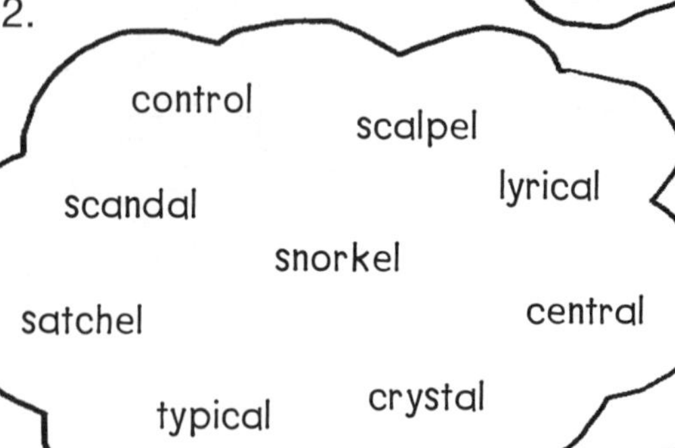

3.

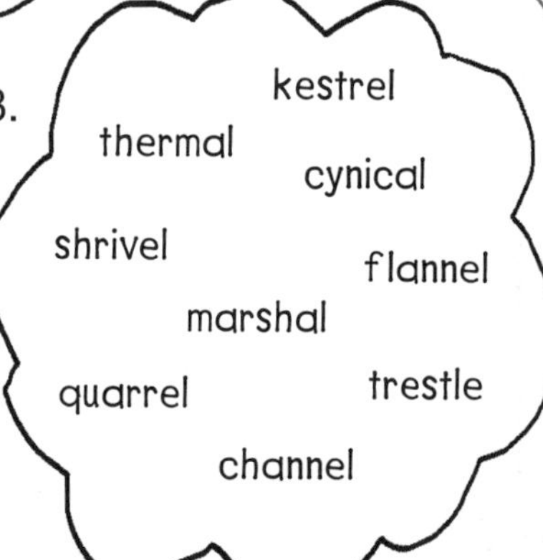

Puzzle Pointer

Look at the letters that make up each word. Vehicle is the odd word out because it has three of these kinds of letter – the other words have two.

The mightiest picture

Can you guess what common sayings these pictures show? Write your answers in the boxes.

1. Don't ☐☐☐ ☐☐ ☐☐☐ ☐☐☐☐☐.

2. The ☐☐☐☐☐ ☐☐ ☐☐☐ ☐☐☐☐.

3. Take ☐☐☐ ☐☐☐☐ ☐☐ ☐☐☐ ☐☐☐☐☐.

4. Too ☐☐☐☐ ☐☐☐☐☐ ☐☐☐☐☐ ☐☐☐ ☐☐☐☐☐.

Tricky

91 Word pyramid 3

Write the answers to the clues in the pyramid. All the answers end in the word **ant**.

Tricky

Clues

1. Small crawling insect that lives in large groups.
2. Breathe quickly and loudly, with your mouth open.
3. On a slope.
4. Not occupied.
5. Small, dried black grape, often used in cakes.
6. Be powerful and have influence over others (begins with **d**).
7. Substance people use on their body to hide or prevent sweat smells.
8. Go here to eat a meal that is cooked and served on the premises.

92 Picture this 3

Can you guess the tricky words shown in these illustrations? Unscramble the letters to work out the remainder of the word after the first letter, and write the word.

1. d isguise (gisseui)
2. e __________ (ssamaberrd)
3. g __________ (itafrfi)
4. j __________ (yellewer)
5. l __________ (repoda)
6. y __________ (chat)

93 Missing creatures 2

Read the clues for each group and guess the name of a creature that can be added to the letters to make three words. The name of the creature can be added before, after or in the middle of the letters, but you cannot change the order of the letters.

1.

Nectar-feeding insect with brightly coloured wings.	butter	butterfly
Hair that is fine and difficult to control.	away	flyaway
Ceremonial flight of aircraft over a given area.	-past	fly-past

Tricky

2.

A view from high above.	's-eye	
Observing this creature in their natural environment.	watching	
Small beetle, usually red or yellow, with black spots.	lady	

3.

Angry or bad-tempered expression.	sl	
Lacks courage.	ard	
Man who rides on horseback to herd cattle.	boy	

4.

Humorous drawing or description that exaggerates someone to be funny.	cariure	
Magazine or booklet that contains a list of items for sale.	alogue	
Competition in which athletes compete in ten events.	dehlon	

Help Tabitha find her way to the treasure. She must follow the words in alphabetical order and can only move up, right, left or down one rectangle at a time. Her first move is shown.

treat	champion	tortoise	treasure
trouble	ceiling	treacle	treason
toffee	tongue	tonsils	tighten
tempting	territory	tango	beautiful
tentacle	terrible	tangle	furniture
temptation	tantrum	musician	temple
temporary	temperature	temper	tadpole
tarragon	technique	television	tasteful
teaspoon ↑	technology	telegraph	teacher
Tabitha	something	somewhere	stampede

Tricky

95 What comes next 4?

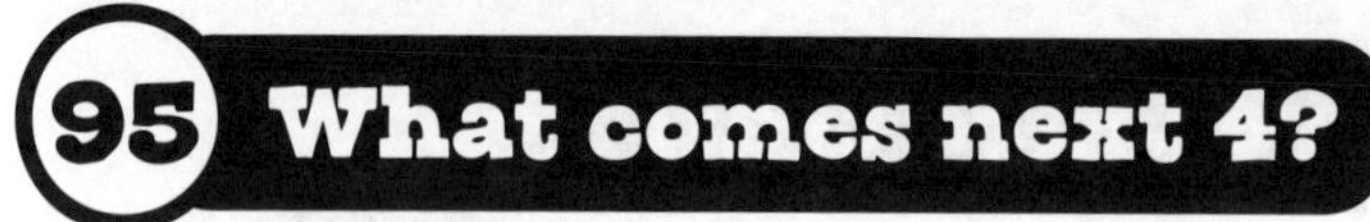

Can you guess the sequence this group of words follows? Write two more words that could be added to the sequence in the big stars.

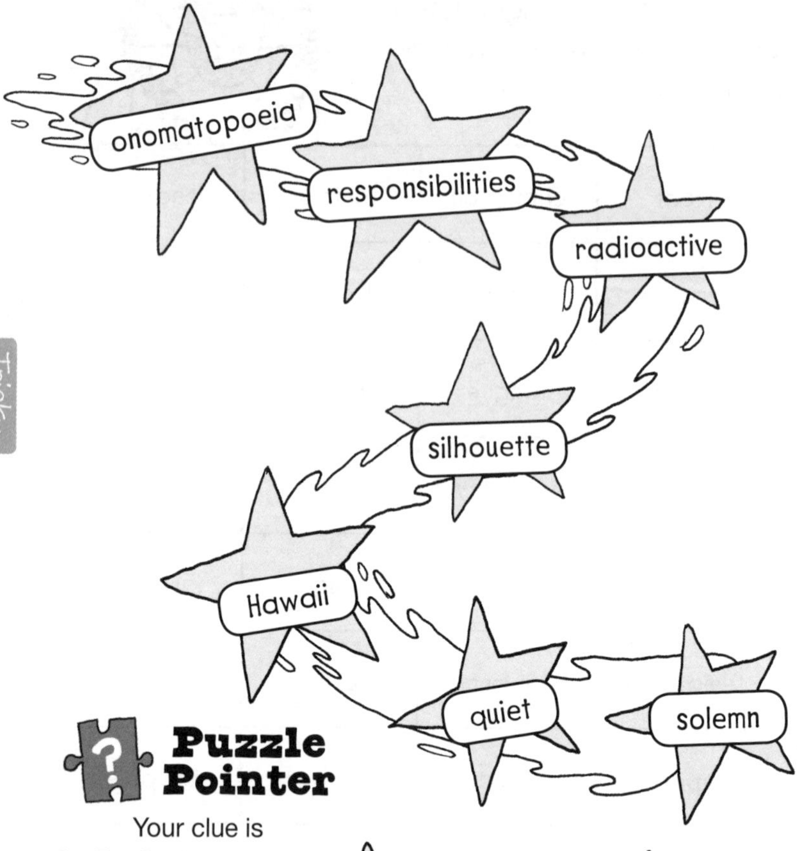

onomatopoeia
responsibilities
radioactive
silhouette
Hawaii
quiet
solemn

Puzzle Pointer

Your clue is
8 – 7 – 6 – 5 – 4 – 3 – 2...

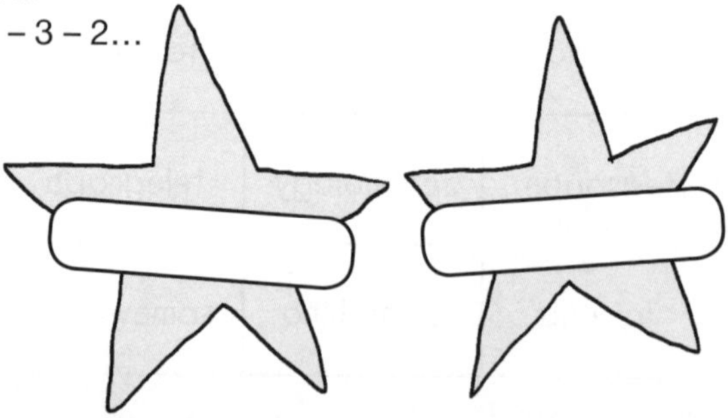

96 Feeding time

Rohit Robot will spontaneously combust unless he is quickly fed his favourite oil. His oil contains the letters in the word **spontaneous**. Rohit needs a dose of 8 **five-letter words** and 12 **four-letter words** made up from these letters. Find and write the words Rohit needs. But no plurals as these will make him sick!

Tricky

Dose of 8 five-letter words:

spoon

Dose of 12 four-letter words:

oops

97 Seeing double

The two words missing in each sentence below are spelt the same but have different meanings. Read each sentence and fill in the missing words. Then find and cross off one of each word in the word search.

1. Jade felt ___bitter___ that hers was the only sparkling water with a sharp, ___bitter___ lemon taste.
2. As part of the PE ________ , Haru ran the ________ in a record-breaking 30 minutes.
3. A tall, long-necked ________ flew by as we watched a towering metal ________ pick up a whole truck.
4. Zach crunched on the hard ________ of his bread as he read about Earth's outer layer called the ________ .
5. A single, long ________ fell in my eye as the rain ________ed hard against the window.
6. Sasha began writing his thank-you ________ with the capital ________ 'T'.
7. In her lesson, the ________ learnt how the size of the eye's ________ changes in different light conditions.
8. The long, reptilian ________ hissed, zig-zagged and ________d across the field.
9. The horses' wooden ________ wasn't blown over in the storm, as it was strong and ________ .
10. His story was nail-biting and ________ , and written in the past ________ .

Tricky

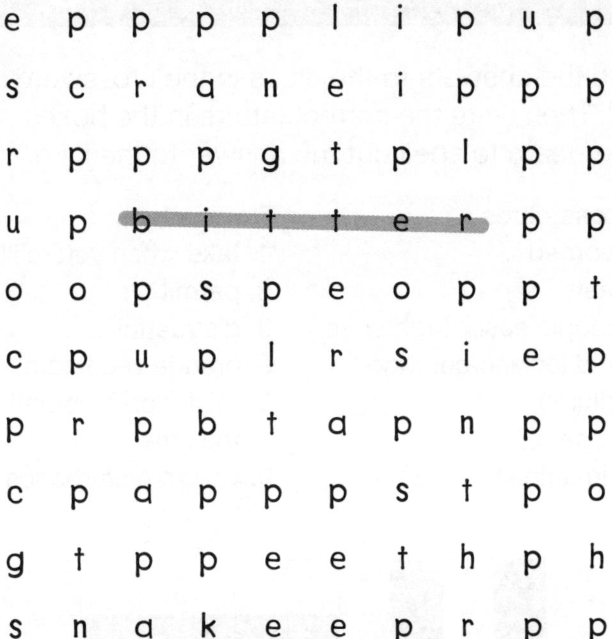

When you have found all of the words, cross off all the pesky leftover letter ‘p’s. Then write the remaining letters, in order, in the answer boxes below to complete the joke.

Tricky

Write the answers to the clues in the crossword grid. Then write the correct letters in the boxes underneath to spell out the answer to the joke.

Across clues
2. worried
4. tasty
7. people easily frightened and lacking courage (plural)
8. huge
10. imaginary

Down clues
1. take when you're ill
2. permit
3. distrustful
5. orange vegetable
6. think about something all the time
9. violent disturbance

Tricky

What do you call a fake noodle?

An G10 E7 J4 F4 H5 F8 D1 !

99 McFlannery's flyshoes

This advert needs editing before it goes to print. Can you help by unscrambling the letters of the words in brackets and writing the correct spellings on the lines?

MCFLANNERY'S FLYSHOES – THERE'S NO BETTER WAY TO TRAVEL!

Does it take you a (nomilil) ______________ hours to travel to school?

Are you tired of sitting at the back of the school bus, in (ssmavei) ______________ traffic queues?

Or does the walk to school seem to get (ronelg) ______________ every day?

Well, now you can leave all that hassle behind and literally take off with a pair of McFlannery's (santtifca) ______________ Flyshoes!

Simply slide your feet into the shoes, clip the buckles, flick the switch... and be prepared for the (dire fo uyor file) ____________________________!

These hassle-free Flyshoes are so easy to look after. Just plug them into a (rachgign) ______________ point after every ten hours of use.

And priced at only £99 a pair, they're the bargain of the (truceny) ______________!

Hurry and order your Flyshoes (dimetimelay) ____________________ before they're sold out!

Tricky

100 Double trouble

All these missing words have two meanings. Read each pair of definitions and write in the word that they both describe. Then write all the first letters of your word answers, in order, to spell out the name given to a word with two meanings.

1. Unit to measure a horse's height.
   A part of the body. ______________
2. A colour.
   A fruit. ______________
3. Unwilling to share.
   A number that is the average of a set of numbers. ______________
4. A thing.
   Disagree with. ______________
5. Type of number less than zero.
   If someone is this, they focus on the bad things. ______________
6. Wild ox.
   Trivial ongoing conversation. yak
7. You're in this if you're angry and irritable.
   The atmosphere or tone of something such as music. ______________

A ☐ ☐ ☐ ☐ ☐ y ☐ is a word that has two meanings.

Tricky

101 Blast off!

Alien Oughty McNoughty needs help to launch her spaceship. Answer the clues, then write your answers in alphabetical order in the launch spiral to help Oughty McNoughty blast off. Every answer contains the letter string **ough**.

Clues

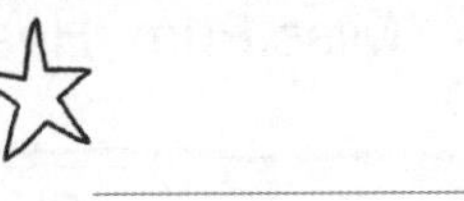

You may have this with a cold. ____________

Strong. ____________

Careful; doesn't leave anything out. ____________

Farm machine. ____________

Tree branch. ____________

Spongy mixture baked into bread. ____________

Go in one side and out the other. ____________

Town or district. borough

Tricky

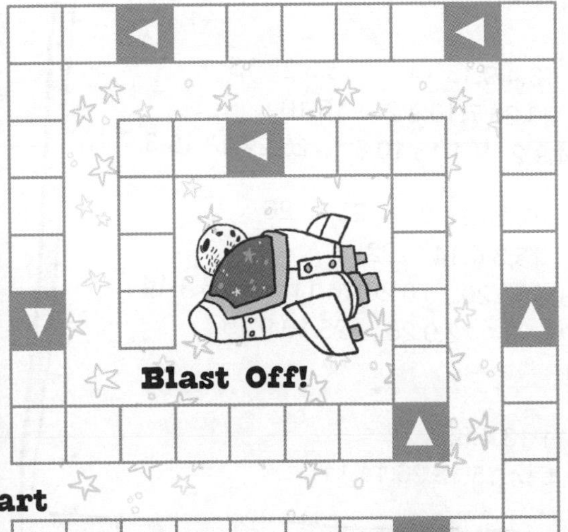

Puzzle Pointer

Some words may be written backwards!

102 Pupil super sleuth

A pupil has found a teacher's text from the headmistress, but it's in code as all the letters have been changed to numbers. The pupil knows which letters some of the numbers stand for as she has guessed that the last two lines of number reads, 'Miss Prim, Headmistress'.

15.10 22.7.7 15.26.22.24.3.26.13.14,

22.24.24.10.13.25.4.9.2 15.10 22 8.20.15.3,
22 3.22.4.13.20, 15.10.10.15.3.7.26.14.14
23.26.22.14.15 11.22.15.13.10.7.14
15.3.26 14.24.3.10.10.7 22.15 9.4.2.3.15.
4 25.4.14.8.4.14.14.26.25 15.3.26
14.15.10.13.20, 16.9.15.4.7 15.3.26
24.22.13.26.15.22.6.26.13 1.10.16.9.25
14.10.8.26 26.9.10.13.8.10.16.14,
8.16.25.25.20
1.10.10.15.11.13.4.9.15.14 15.3.22.15
25.10.9'15 23.26.7.10.9.2 15.10
22.9.20.15.3.4.9.2 1.13.10.8 26.22.13.15.3.

15.3.26 11.10.7.4.24.26 22.13.26
8.22.6.4.9.2 15.3.4.14 22
11.13.4.10.13.4.15.20. 6.26.26.11 15.3.4.14
14.26.24.13.26.15 22.9.25 25.10.9'15
11.22.9.4.24!

8.4.14.14 11.13.4.8,
3.26.22.25.8.4.14.15.13.26.14.14

Tricky

Can you decode the rest of the text and write what it says below?

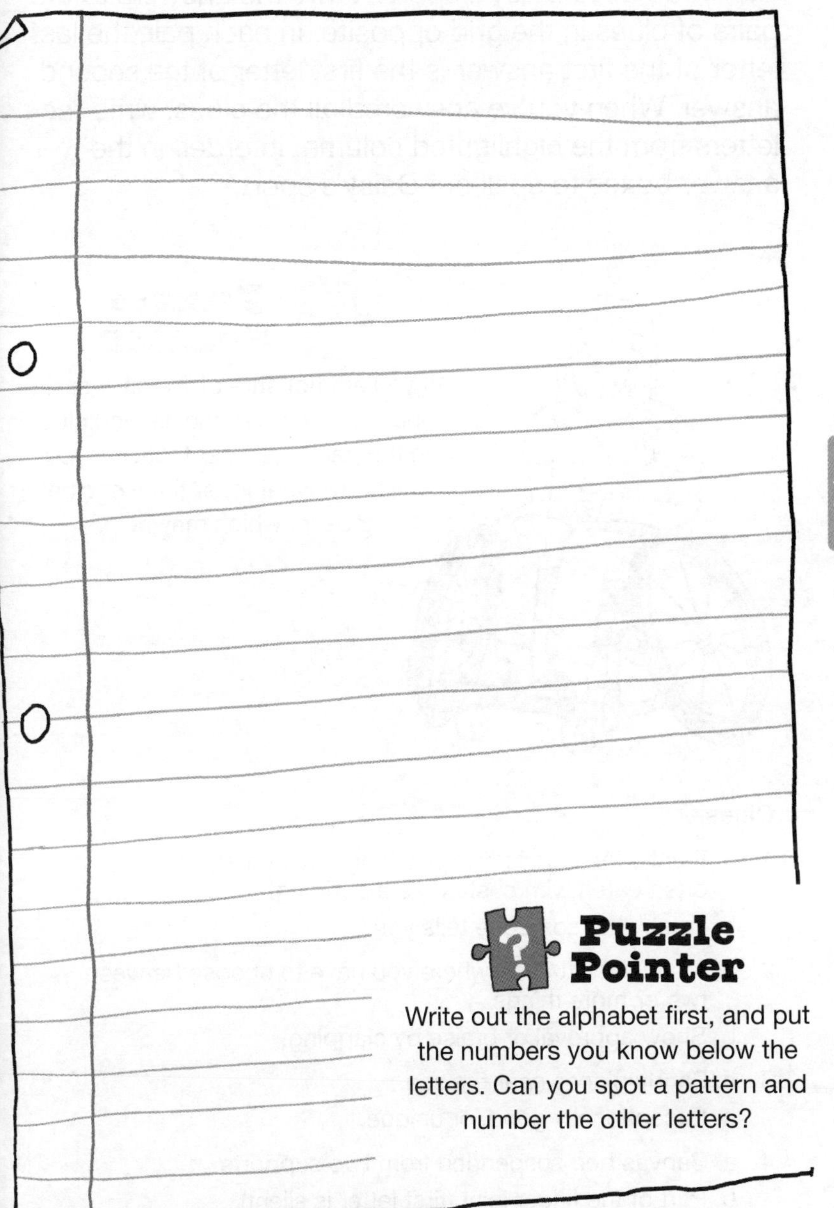

Puzzle Pointer

Write out the alphabet first, and put the numbers you know below the letters. Can you spot a pattern and number the other letters?

103 Super sport

Can you guess Daisy's sport? Write the answers to the pairs of clues in the grid opposite. In each pair, the last letter of the first answer is the first letter of the second answer. When you've answered all the clues, write the letters from the highlighted column, in order, in the answer boxes to spell out Daisy's sport.

Puzzle Pointer

If you are not sure of the answer to one clue, go on to the second clue in the pair. If you get that clue you will know what letter the first clue ends in, which may help.

Tricky

Clues

1 a. Plant with large leaves and long red stems; often eaten with custard as a pudding.
  b. Trust what someone tells you.

2 a. A difficult situation where you have to choose between two or more things.
  b. Show approval or praise by clapping.

3 a. Sandy places near the sea.
  b. Exceptionally good, or unique.

4 a. Canvas bed suspended from two supports.
  b. Part of the finger joint (first letter is silent).

5 a. Calculate the size of something using a ruler.
  b. Time at the end of the day.

6 a. An idea in your mind (begins with **th**).
  b. Mental or emotional strain (rhymes with **mention**).

7 a. Interrupt someone; make noise that bothers someone (begins with **d**).
  b. A conjunction meaning **for the reason that**.

8 a. Group of letters, numbers or other symbols that represent a scientific or mathematical rule.
  b. Details of a place where someone lives.

9 a. Occurring at the beginning (begins with **i**).
  b. Suitcases or other bags you may take on holiday.

10 a. Delightful in a way that seems out-of-this-world (begins with **m**).
  b. A quiet, gentle song, sung to send a child to sleep.

				a.							b.		
1.													
2.	d	i	l	e	m	m	a	p	p	l	a	u	d
3.													
4.													
5.													
6.													
7.													
8.													
9.													
10.													

Daisy's sport is wheelchair ____ ____ ____ ____ ____ ____ ____ ____ ____ ____ .

104 Odd one out 3

Can you guess the odd word out in each of these three groups of words? The first one has been done for you. Look for the same pattern in the two other groups.

1.

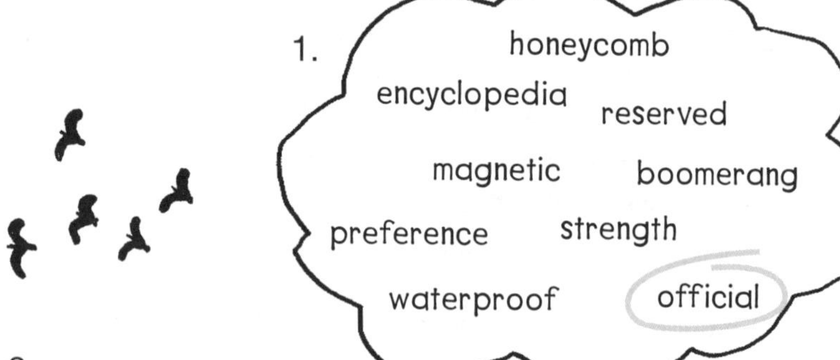

2.

3.

circumference
compulsory
spectacular
interview
menu
independent
archaeopteryx
satnav
suspicious

Look at the last letter of each word. See if you can spot any order.

Crossword challenge 3

Are you ready for a challenge? The answer to each clue is its opposite word. When you've worked out these antonyms, write them in the crossword grid. Then write the correct letters in the boxes underneath to spell out the answer to the joke.

Across clues
2. ease
5. synonym
6. cheap
9. dirtier

Down clues
1. safe
3. seldom
4. shy
7. war
8. exit

What stays in the corner, yet travels all over the world?

A [A9] [E3] [C7] [I3] [C5] !

Tricky

The bold words in this top secret memo are the answers to the clues opposite. Can you fit the answers into the word grid?

CONFIDENTIAL MEMO

Dear Colleague,

It is **essential** that under no circumstances must the contents of this **confidential** memo be revealed to the public.

Our **Special** Investigation Services (SIS) has provided information on the latest developments in **artificial** intelligence. The **initial** results show that advances are happening at a **torrential** pace, as robots are rapidly learning to do most things that humans can do, and have the **potential** to do even more superhuman things in the future.

Our report is **impartial**, as we are not involved in any of the tests and our well-respected organization has superb **credentials**. Additionally, its timing is **providential** as we move further into the 21st century.

The official statement that we will be releasing to the public is:

"Research into artificial intelligence is crucial as we look for ways that it can be **beneficial** to human life."

Yours faithfully,

Wanda Bright

Commander-in-Chief, SIS

Clues

1. Exceptionally good.
2. To be kept secret.
3. Created by humans and not found in nature.
4. Previous achievements or training.
5. Favourable or advantageous.
6. Occurring at the beginning.
7. Extremely important.
8. Not directly involved so can give a fair opinion.
9. Lucky because it happens at the right time.
10. Can develop into something in the future.
11. Falling rapidly and in large quantities.
    (Usually refers to rain)

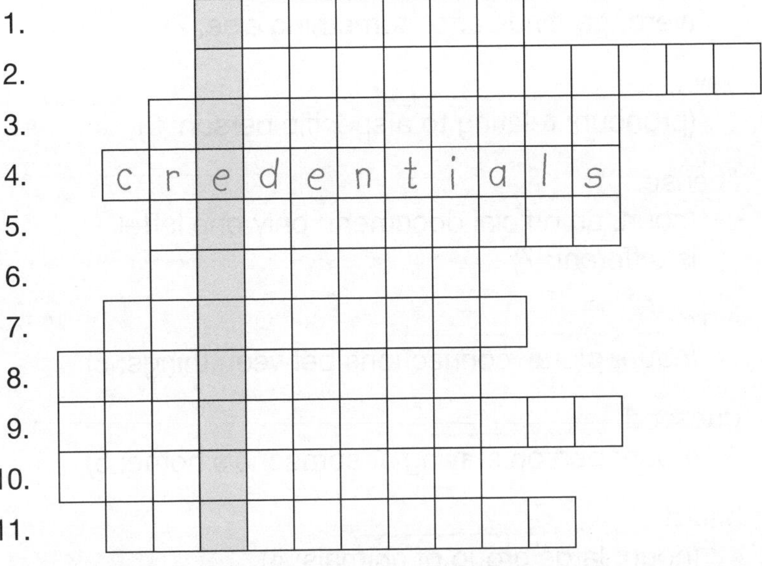

Write the letters in the shaded column, in order, in the boxes below to spell out the answer to the joke.

What do you get when you cross a computer with a lifeguard?

A !

107 Sound twins

Remember homophones sound the same but have different meanings and can have different spellings. Read the clues in brackets and work out the homophones or near homophones for each of these words, then fit your answers in the word grid.

Clues

prophesy: prophecy
(noun: prediction of the future; 8)

precede: ____________________
(verb: continue after something else; 7)

yew: ____________________
(pronoun: relating to a specific person; 3)

license: ____________________
(noun: an official document; only one letter is different; 7)

lynx: ____________________
(noun, plural: connections between things; 5)

guessed: ____________________
(noun: person staying at someone's home; 5)

heard: ____________________
(noun: large group of animals; 4)

earn: ____________________
(noun: container used for ashes; 3)

sighed: ____________________
(noun: flat, outer surface of an object; 4)

principal: ____________________
(noun: belief you have about the way you should behave; 9)

ode: ____________________
(verb, past tense: something that should have been paid; 4)

two: ____________________
(preposition: moving towards; 2)

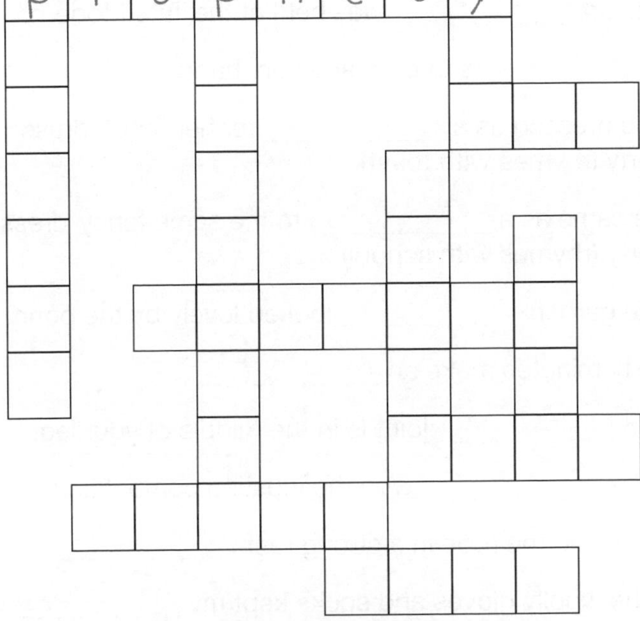

Don't get caught out by **precede**, as it sounds slightly different to its partner.

108 Whopping word search

The missing words in these sentences all contain a silent letter and are in alphabetical order. Fill in the missing words, then find and cross off these words in the word search. You will find them written forwards, backwards, up, down or diagonally.

1. The crispy leaves fell off the trees in ____________ .
2. The political party launched their c____________ .
3. The art ____________ was held at the Tate Modern.
4. Exhilarate is to be made very happy.
5. She dressed as a ____________ for her fancy-dress party (rhymes with toast).
6. He came as a ____________ to the same fancy-dress party (rhymes with school).
7. The garden ____________ looked lovely by the pond.
8. Sixty minutes make an ____________ .
9. The ____________ joint is in the middle of your leg.
10. The ____________ won the jousting competition.
11. She tied the rope in a strong reef ____________ .
12. The woolly gloves and socks kept my ____________ warm.
13. A loud ____________ came from the stable.
14. The doctor said her cold had worsened into ____________
15. A p____________ was a flying reptile in the time of the dinosaurs (10 letters).

Tricky

16. The musician had great r______________ .

17. It takes ______________ to tango.

18. The ______________ surfaced in the ocean to breathe through its blowhole.

p	t	e	r	a	n	o	d	o	n
n	r	t	s	s	u	e	w	g	i
e	x	h	i	b	i	t	i	o	n
u	l	g	y	v	m	a	u	g	e
m	r	i	w	t	p	i	n	m	h
o	t	n	h	m	h	o	l	g	n
n	o	k	a	g	m	m	h	h	h
i	n	c	l	e	o	o	l	o	d
a	k	n	e	e	u	e	u	s	n
e	x	h	i	l	a	r	a	t	e

Write down the letters that are left over, in order, to fill in the missing words in this expression.

Speech is ______________ **,**

but silence is ______________ **.**

Tricky

109 Quick quiz 3

Are you ready to test your quiz powers and see how much you remember from the tricky puzzles? Circle the letter next to the correct answer to each of these questions. Then write the letters beside your answers in the answer boxes, in order, to spell out the name of an animal that has been trained to hunt for one of the world's most expensive foods.

1. This person is careful and doesn't leave anything out.

   T thoughtful **P** careless

2. If you're mistaken, you are **barking up the wrong** ____________.

   R tree **O** goalpost

3. Which word is an antonym of **expensive**?

   U cheap **O** pricey

4. This word comes after **tentacle** in alphabetical order.

   F terrible **D** tempting

5. Which word is a homophone for **guest**?

   L visitor **F** guessed

6. This letter is a silent letter in the word **solemn**.

   E m **L** n

7. This word can be written as the digit **0**.

Y eight **E** nought

8. What animal can be added to the letters **sel** to describe a person who doesn't think of others.

D fish **C** owl

9. Which word belongs to this group of words: **upstairs, everywhere**.

A yesterday **O** outside

10. Which word completes the expression: **A picture paints a thousand** ____________?

T people **G** words

Tricky

The animal is a

☐☐☐☐☐☐☐ ☐☐☐.

Puzzle power!

Your puzzle power must be nearly at boiling point by now. Check the answers at the end of the book and add up how many tricky puzzles you got right. Score 2 for each fully correct puzzle, and 1 if you got some of the puzzle right. Then write down your total and read on to discover your puzzle power…

My puzzle power score is  **.**

Puzzle power score 1–25

Grab a dictionary and a thesaurus to pump up your puzzle power and go over some of the tricky puzzles you found most challenging.

Puzzle power score 26–49

Your puzzle power is simmering. Have another go at some of the more tricky puzzles to get it to boiling point.

Puzzle power score 50+

You are a puzzle superstar and there are no limits to your puzzle power! Next stop, see if you can tackle *Bond Brain Training: Logic Puzzles* and *Brain Training: Number Puzzles*.

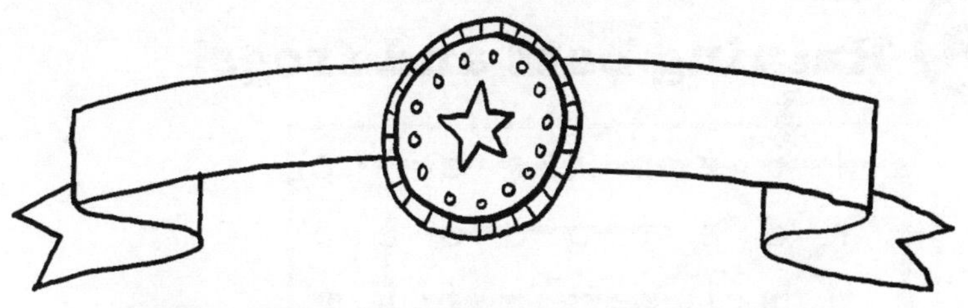

Answers

Warm-up puzzles

PAGE 6

1 Just joking!

Which athlete is warm in winter?

A long jumper!

PAGE 7

2 Raining bats and frogs!

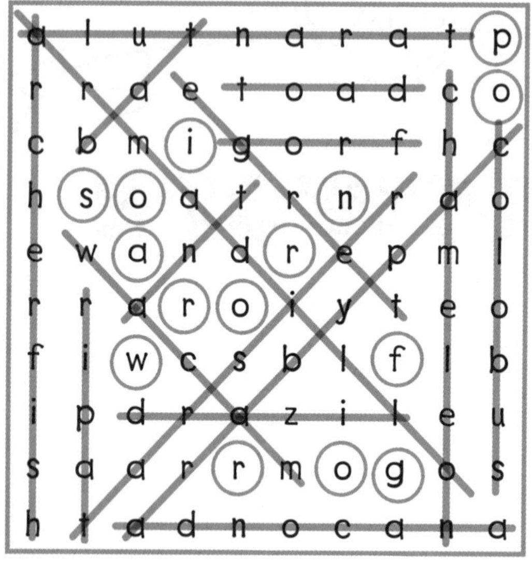

The creature you wouldn't want to touch is a **poison arrow frog** (also called a poison dart frog). Some species are deadly poisonous and the poison from one tiny frog can kill ten adult men!

PAGE 8

3 Pick up pens

Talia's contribution to drama this year has been **tremendous**.

PAGE 9

4 The tale of Charlie Crumb

There once was a plumber to everyone,
Who went by the name of Charlie Crumb.
One day Charlie saw his good friend **John**,
Who spotted that Charlie was feeling **numb**.

Charlie had finished with sinks and loos,
And was looking forward to getting out.
But as he was leaving for his world **cruise**,
He wasn't so sure and began to **doubt**.

"I'm scared," said Charlie to his good **friend**.
"Can I do it? I don't really **know**,
Problems in houses are what I mend."
"Relax," said John. "And just take it slow."

So Charlie packed his bags for summer,
And went off to sail along the **Rhine**.
And ever since he's been a **plumber**,
Happily working for a big cruise line.

PAGE 10

Cheeky chef

ketchup, **chickpeas**, **chocolate**, ostrich, **chilli**, **chicken**, quiche, gnocchi, **cheese**, **chips**, **chives**, spinach, **chorizo**, enchilada, **cherries**, **chestnuts**, artichoke.

Only the words in bold should be circled.

PAGE 11

6 Shocking selfie

z, y, x, w, v, u, t, s, r, q, p, o, n, m, l, k, j, i, h, g, f, e, d, c, b, a.

The dot-to-dot cellfie picture reveals that the prisoner is an **alien**!

PAGE 12

7 Message in a bottle

The message in a bottle reads: **Where do bees go on holiday? Stingapore!**

The code for the joke: Where do pepperonis go on holiday? The Leaning Tower of Pizza!

PAGE 13

8 Beside the seashore

<table>
<tr><td>s</td><td></td><td></td><td></td><td></td><td></td><td></td><td></td><td></td><td></td><td></td></tr>
<tr><td>h</td><td></td><td></td><td></td><td></td><td></td><td></td><td></td><td></td><td>s</td><td></td></tr>
<tr><td>r</td><td></td><td>s</td><td></td><td>l</td><td>o</td><td>b</td><td>s</td><td>t</td><td>e</td><td>r</td></tr>
<tr><td>i</td><td></td><td>t</td><td></td><td></td><td></td><td>a</td><td></td><td></td><td>a</td><td></td></tr>
<tr><td>m</td><td></td><td>a</td><td></td><td></td><td></td><td>r</td><td></td><td></td><td>w</td><td></td></tr>
<tr><td>p</td><td>e</td><td>r</td><td>i</td><td>w</td><td>i</td><td>n</td><td>k</td><td>l</td><td>e</td><td></td></tr>
<tr><td></td><td></td><td>f</td><td></td><td></td><td></td><td>a</td><td></td><td></td><td>e</td><td></td></tr>
<tr><td></td><td></td><td>i</td><td></td><td></td><td></td><td>c</td><td></td><td></td><td>d</td><td></td></tr>
<tr><td></td><td></td><td>s</td><td>c</td><td>a</td><td>l</td><td>l</td><td>o</td><td>p</td><td></td><td></td></tr>
<tr><td></td><td></td><td>h</td><td></td><td></td><td></td><td>e</td><td></td><td></td><td></td><td></td></tr>
</table>

What do you call a greedy fish?

Selfish!

PAGE 14

9 What am I 1?

What is a prisoner's favourite food?

Cellery!

The answer is a pun on the proper spelling of the word celery.

PAGE 15

10 Tiny trail

tiny →	small	jumbo	whopping
enormous	↓ minute	huge	vast
big	↓ wee →	little →	miniscule
tremendous	monstrous	oversize	↓ teeny
grand	mini ←	teeny-weeny ←	↓ microscopic
great	↓ dinky	bumper	towering
massive	↓ pocket-sized →	miniature →	petite

PAGE 16

11 Word square 1

Here are some of the words you can make out of the letters a, l, c, o, m, e, h, e, n:

Four-letter words: **ache, calm, came, clam, clan, coal, come, each, heel, helm, hole, home, lace, lame, lane, lean, loan, male, mane, meal, mean, moan, mole, name**

Five-letter words: **clean, clone, leach, lemon, melon**

Nine-letter word: **chameleon**

Did you spot the nine-letter word? Well done if you did, and if you found any other words.

PAGE 17

12 Solar system search

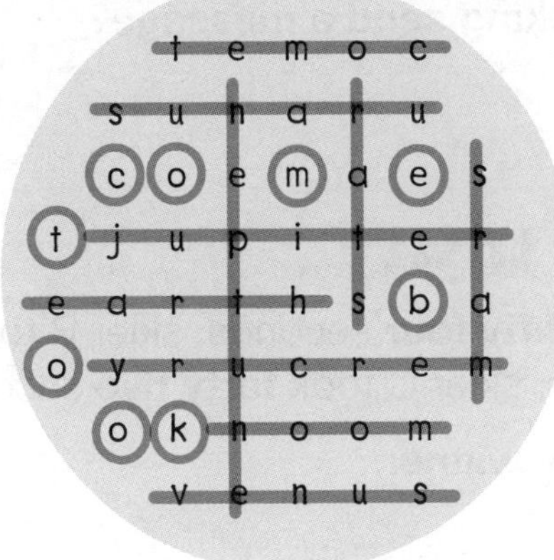

What is a planet's favourite thing to read?

A comet book!

PAGES 18–19

13 Dazzle Dance Show

You were full of drama like **a diva**.

It was as graceful as **a beautiful swan**.

It was so slow like you were **stuck in mud**.

It was as scary as **a rollercoaster ride**.

It was as entertaining as **a clown**.

You were as quick as **lightning**.

Any sentences that include a simile and make sense are fine. You may have included these similes: as glamorous as a film star; glitzy like a disco ball; as flashy as exploding fireworks; as dull as watching paint dry; as comical as a donkey; like a vision from the stars.

PAGE 20

Picture puzzle 1

How did a Viking send a message?

Norse code!

PAGE 21

Letter trail

Skier A took **fifty four** seconds, skier B took **forty four** seconds, skier C took **forty five** seconds.

Skier B is the winner.

PAGE 22

Word wall 1

The following bricks can be used in the word wall: **spectacular, amusing, charming, fabulous, fantastic, incredible, sensational, enjoyable, wonderful.** These words are all synonyms of entertaining, exciting, delightful, dramatic and thrilling.

PAGE 23

The big picture

1. **Couch potato**, 2. A **long face**, 3. **Cut corners**, 4. A **wet blanket**, 5. I'll **eat my hat**, 6. The **dog ate my homework**.

PAGES 24–5

Jupiter's stars

Here are some of the words you may have made: **supersonic, superhero, superhuman, supercool, immature, impatient, inappropriate, insane,**

inhuman, dislike, outdated, uncool, unruly, unusual.

PAGE 26

19 What am I 2?

What do you call a funny mountain?

Hill-arious!

The answer is a pun on the proper spelling of the word hilarious.

PAGE 27

20 Slimy code

1. **nose hairs**, 2. **pickled toe**, 3. **finger wart**, 4. **chocolate**, 5. **blue tongue**, 6. **fish burps**.

PAGE 28

21 Picture this 1

1. **super**model, 2. **sub**marine, 3. **super**market, 4. **sub**tract, 5. **anti**clockwise, 6. **anti**septic.

Other words you could illustrate include: submerge, subtitle, subzero; superb, supercool, superhero, superior, supernatural, superstar; antisocial. There are lots more, too!

PAGE 29

22 Healing words

yachtsman, **m**oonlight, **o**vercome, **u**nderwear, **l**ifestyle, **d**aydream, **a**irport, **b**lockbuster, **r**iverbank, **e**arphones, **d**ishwasher.

The Ancient Egyptians put **mouldy bread** on their

cuts to heal them. The fungi and bacteria in the mould killed the bacteria that cause the infection. But don't try it at home! Modern penicillin came from mould.

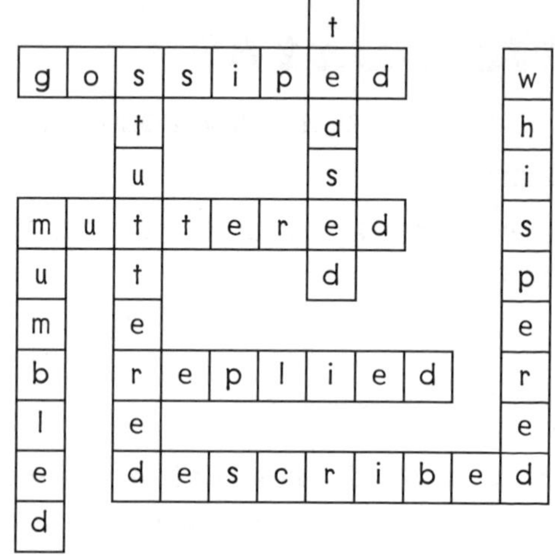

Some words will fit in more than one sentence. Here are some suggestions…

1. "I'm sorry that I rode your precious bike," **muttered** Liam.
2. "I d ... don't think I can climb down as I'm sc ... sc ... ared of heights!" **stuttered** Amy.
3. "My gorgeous pug is brown, two years old, and called Scotty," **described** Sasha.
4. "Did you hear that Teddy had his picture taken by the local paper?" **gossiped** Jess.
5. "It's lovely to see you, too," **replied** Mohammed.
6. "If you're nice to me, I'll let you sit here," **teased** Alice.
7. "Shh, be quiet," **whispered** Hideko.

8. “I don’t like playing football in the rain,” **mumbled** Alfie.

PAGE 32

24 Dominque’s boutique

quiz, **squeaker**, **racquet**, quick, **macaque** (a monkey), squirm, **croquet**, equal, quack, **queen**, **antique**, aquarium, **barbeque**, **marquee**, **bouquet**, earthquake, **plaque**.

Only the words in bold should be circled.

PAGE 33

25 Arctic animals

For the code, write the alternate **odd** letters in order first (the 1st, 3rd, 5th, 7th and so on to the end of the word/s). Then go back and write the alternate **even** letters (the 2nd, 4th, 6th, 8th and so on).

1. **walrus**, 2. **polar bear**, 3. **albatross**, 4. **beluga whale**, 5. **Arctic fox**, 6. **narwhal**, 7. **Emperor penguin**, 8. **puffin**, 9. **reindeer**, 10. **Weddell seal**.

The illustrated Arctic animal is a ***narwhal***.

PAGE 34

26 Tongue-tied

Try out your tongue-twisters on your friends.

PAGE 35

27 Music trail

g r a **n** e l m **o** r t a **t** r u s **e** g o n **s**

What makes songs but never sings?

Notes!

PAGES 36–7

Word sandwiches 1

1. quick**sand**, **sand**castle, 2. wall**paper**, **paper**back, 3. score**card**, **card**board, 4. net**ball**, **ball**boy, 5. dog**house**, **house**boat, 6. bird**bath**, **bath**tub, 7. horse**back**, **back**ground, 8. fire**work**, **work**man, 9. cry**baby**, **baby**sitter, 10. back**hand**, **hand**stand.

PAGE 38

29 What comes next 1?

All the words begin with the prefix **dis**. Any word beginning with **dis** is correct here, for example: discourage, dishonest, discomfort and so on.

PAGE 39

30 Rhymes and climbs

1. **trick**, 2. **crick**, 3. **click**, 4. **slick**, 5. **flick**.

6. **fable**, 7. **gable**, 8. **sable**, 9. **table**, 10. **cable**.

PAGE 40

31 Spell it out!

1. **business**, 2. **calendar**, 3. **island**, 4. **knowledge**, 5. **friend**, 6. **occasional**, 7. **potatoes**, 8. **separate**.

Your mnemonic can be anything, but an example is the following: **m**unch **n**uts **e**legantly, **m**unch **o**nions **n**aughtily, **i**n **c**hoir.

PAGE 41

Word wall 2

The antonyms are: **villain–hero, quiet–noisy, public–private, create–destroy, descend–ascend, sharp–**

blunt, wealth–poverty, freeze–boil, bold–cautious.

The odd words out are: **furthest** and **last**. Their antonyms are: **furthest–nearest, last–first.**

PAGES 42–3

33 *The Daily Giggle*

The words that tell the reader it's about comedy are in bold.

The Daily ***Giggle***

A **fun** night out

Stand-up **comic** Badeea Badour performed in front of a sell-out crowd at The Big Arena last Saturday. She had the crowd in the palm of her hand with her **hilarious** opening **joke** about supermarket self-service checkouts. Her **witty** and **playful** exchanges with members from the audience had even the most solemn people cracking a **laugh**.

The improvisation section of Badeea's act was particularly **amusing**, with the audience shouting out random, **humorous** topics for her to act out. The whole evening was a **jovial** night out and everyone left feeling **cheerful**.

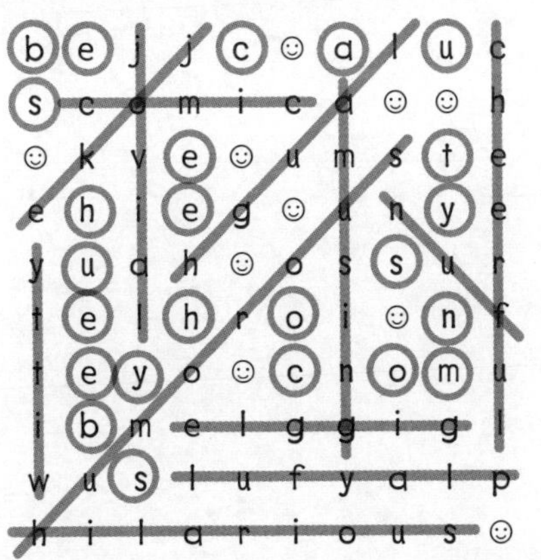

Why do bees have sticky hair?

Because they use honey combs!

The slipper thief

The 11 adjectives are in bold.

At two o'clock yesterday afternoon, my colleague and I arrived at the scene of the robbery. I ordered the staff to close the shop, and we commenced the **mammoth** task of searching for evidence. I found exhibit A: a **triangular** tag from a **large** dog's collar with the name Muncher on it.

I soon met the owner of this collar, and the thief, too. Behind the counter, next to a **monumental** pile of slippers, and with a slipper in his mouth, was Muncher. I was **nervous** and my mouth was **dry**, but my **stalwart** colleague helped me to coax Muncher away from the slippers. We didn't have to worry, as Muncher was **tame**, although he looked rather **thin**.

We would like to thank the staff for their **tremendous** help. We are looking for Muncher's owners, but for now he is at the police station tucking into a **mountainous** bowl of food.

What do you do if your dog chews a dictionary?

Take the words out of his mouth!

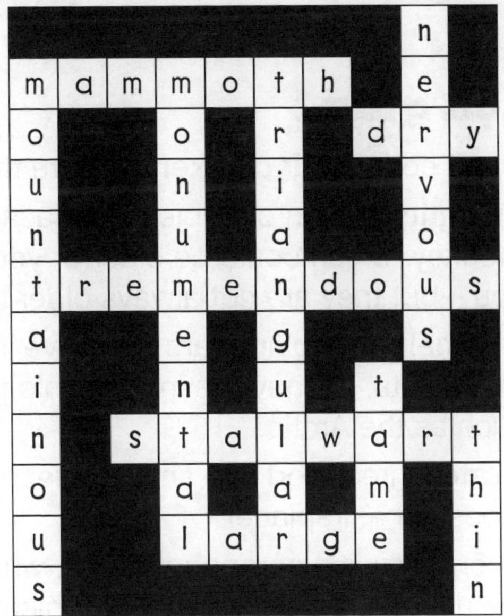

PAGE 46

35 Word pyramid 1

1. **rat**, 2. d**rat**, 3. **rat**io, 4. ka**rat**e, 5. ope**rat**e, 6. g**rat**eful, 7. appa**rat**us, 8. labo**rat**ory.

PAGE 47

36 Crossword challenge 1

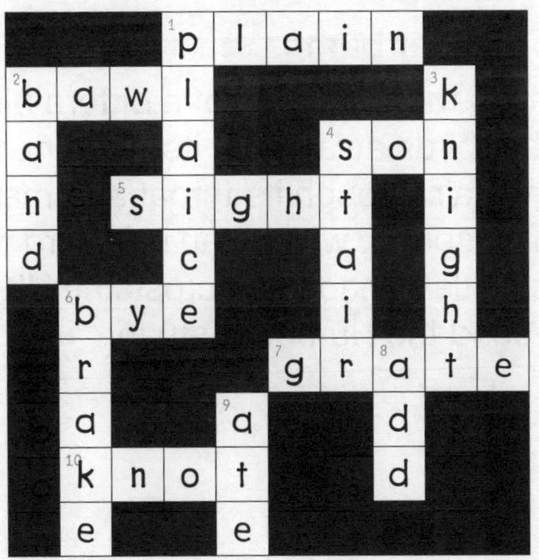

Quick quiz 1

1. **B** Don't count your **chickens** before they hatch.
2. **U** An **antique** is an old object. A macaque is a monkey, which could be older or younger than you – but they are not always older than you.
3. **T** **Chameleon**. Polar bears don't live in rainforests, as they live in very cold places such as the Arctic.
4. **T** **Grate** (shred food into smaller pieces, or the recess of a fireplace).
5. **E** Over**come** is a compound word, which means to succeed in dealing with a problem or being overwhelmed by something.
6. **R** **Microscopic**. Tremendous can mean very large, which is the opposite of tiny.
7. **B** **O** is the fourth vowel in the alphabet.
8. **U** **Island**.
9. **M** **Hero** is an antonym of villain, as it means the opposite.
10. **P** **Lemon**.

The bird is a **butter bump**.

Butter bump is the nickname of a bittern bird. To warn other birds away from its territory, the male bittern pumps air through its throat and makes an odd, booming sound, which can be heard for miles. They live in wetland habitats across the UK, for example around the Humber Estuary.

PAGE 52

38 Riddle time!

What is as big as an elephant but weighs nothing?

Its shadow!

PAGE 53

39 Pick up sticks

What do you get if you cross a cocker spaniel, a poodle and a rooster?

A cockerpoodledoo!

PAGE 54

40 Guess the letter 1

1. Go forwards five letters to **k**. 2. Advance to the next vowel **o**. 3. The missing word is **rhyme**, which has **5** letters. Go back to **j**. 4. Jump backwards **5** letters to **e**. 5. Slide forwards **21** letters to **z**. 6. Retreat 20 steps to **f**.

You are back where you started, at the letter **f**.

PAGE 55

41 Picture puzzle 2

What game do space cadets play?

Astronauts and crosses!

The answer is a pun on the proper spelling of the game, *noughts and crosses*.

PAGE 56

Mention the invention!

gyration, fission, **sedation**, infusion, illusion, **lotion**, **rotation**, explosion, **eruption**, corrosion, collision, **radiation**, **vibration**, **medication**, propulsion, **solution**, transmission, **potion**.

Only the words in bold should be circled.

PAGE 57

Word wall 3

The words in the brick wall all end in the letters **ant**. The following bricks can be used: **restaurant, tolerant, participant, triumphant, consonant, significant, pleasant, slant, truant, sergeant, mutant.**

PAGE 58

Word patterns

ought: bought, brought, fought, nought, thought.

ough: although, bough, cough, enough, rough, though, through.

PAGE 59

Pick up swords

Who invented King Arthur's round table?

Sir Cumference!

PAGE 60

Guess the word 1

Akio wants to add the shell with the word **mystery** written on it to his collection.

PAGE 61

47 Word sandwiches 2

1. tomb**stone**, **stone**wall; 2. cart**wheel, wheel**barrow; 3. fire**wood, wood**land; 4. eye**sight, sight**see; 5. wind**screen, screen**play; 6. cat**walk, walk**about; 7. mouth**wash, wash**basin; 8. whole**meal, meal**time; 9. water**fall, fall**out; 10. ball**room, room**mate.

PAGE 62

48 Puzzle muddle

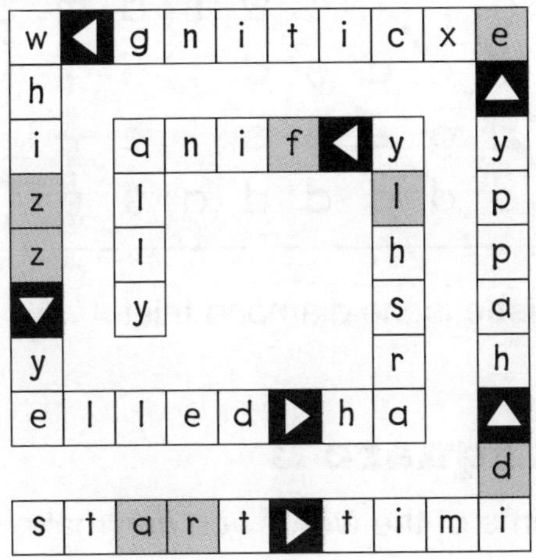

Fergus feels **frazzled**.

PAGE 63

49 Word pyramid 2

1. **sand**, 2. **sand**y, 3. **sand**al, 4. **sand**pit, 5. **sand**wich, 6. **sand**storm, 7. thou**sand**th.

PAGES 64–5

Who done it?

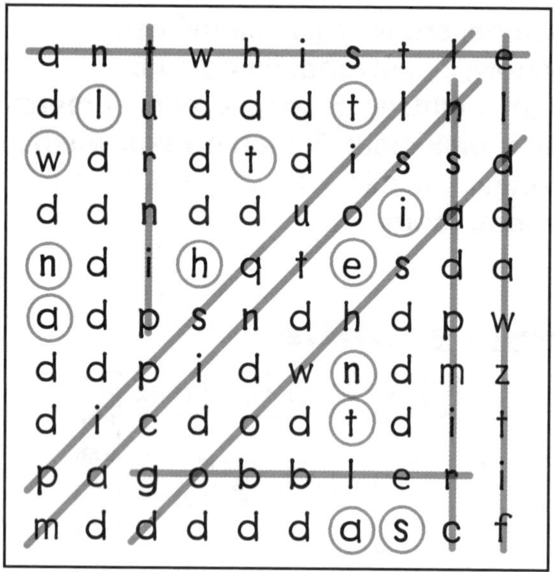

Ant Antwhistle is the diamond thief.

PAGE 66

Word square 2

Here are some of the words you can make out of the letters o, i, t, e, r, o, a, p, n:

Four-letter words: **pair, pare, part, pear, pert, poor, pore, port, rant, rapt, rate, reap, rent, riot, ripe, root, rope, rote, tarn, tear, tern, tore, torn, trap, trip**

Five-letter words: **inter, opera, print, prone, ratio, ripen, train, tripe, troop**

Six-letter words: **orient, parent, patron, pirate, proton, ration**

Seven-letter words: **painter, pointer, portion, protein**

Nine-letter word: **operation**

Did you spot the nine-letter word? Well done if you did, and if you found any other words.

PAGE 67

52 Knight school

1. **bawl!** 2. **rattle!** 3. **clatter!** 4. **neigh!** 5. **screech!** 6. **jangle!** 7. **crackle!** 8. **thwack!**

PAGE 68–9

53 Best Bakes

1. **distasteful** (every letter), 2. **disgusting** (every second letter), 3. **abominable** (every third letter), 4. **repugnant** (every fourth letter), 5. **delightful** (every fifth letter), 6. **loathsome** (every sixth letter), 7. **revolting** (every seventh letter), 8. **shocking** (every eighth letter).

The winning cake is **number 5**.

PAGE 70

Word ladder 1

1. **pane**, 2. **pine**, 3. **fine**, 4. **find**, 5. **bind**, 6. **bond**, 7. **bone**, 8. **done**, 9. **dome**.

PAGE 71

Guess the word 2

The password is **referee**.

PAGES 72–3

56 Perfect Pooches

			h									
			u									
			m		e		f	a	m	o	u	s
			o		n			d				
			r		o			v		c		
		c	o	u	r	a	g	e	o	u	s	
			u		m			n		r		
			s		o			t		i		
					u			u		o		
		b	o	i	s	t	e	r	o	u	s	
								o		s		
								u				
g	l	a	m	o	r	o	u	s				

Why did one of the dogs at Perfect Pooches sweat so much?

Because he was a **hot dog**!

PAGE 74

Find the words

The words are: **live**, **pose**, **gnat**, **eight**, **heart**, **tramp**, **clear**, **cliff**.

PAGE 75

58 Snow scare

Abominable Snowman! The Abominable Snowman, or Yeti, is a mysterious creature who is said to live in the snowy mountains of Asia. Tracks of a huge, big-footed creature have been found in the snow, but no-one has ever proved it exists.

PAGE 76

59 Guess the word 3

The password is **intelligent**.

PAGE 77

60 The bigger picture

1. Don't **let the bedbugs bite**. 2. Let **the cat out of the bag**. 3. Two **heads are better than one**. 4. It's **raining cats and dogs**.

PAGE 78

61 Word ladder 2

1. **stole**, 2. **least**, 3. **steel**, 4. **sweet**, 5. **sweat**, 6. **wheat**, 7. **cheat**.

PAGE 79

62 Picture this 2

1. confiden**tial**, 2. supersti**tious**, 3. ini**tial**, 4. deli**cious**, 5. ambi**tious**, 6. suspi**cious**.

Other words you could illustrate include: gracious, precious, unconscious, cautious, infectious, sequential, palatial, artificial.

PAGES 80–1

63 Mischief-makers

						m			
	m	i	s	c	h	i	e	f	
						s			
				m		e			
				i		r			m
		m	i	s	h	a	p		i
				c		b			s
	m			h		l			c
m	i	s	t	i	m	e			o
	s			e					u
	s			v					n
m	i	s	c	o	n	d	u	c	t
	n			u					
	g			s					

Why did the burglar rob a bakery?

Because he needed the **dough**!

PAGE 82

Password puzzle

The words are: **w**ord, **h**ear, **o**ops, **o**ppose, **p**ride, **E**arth, **e**ast.

The password is **whoopee**!

PAGE 83

65 Roaring names

1. **Tyrannosaurus Rex**, 2. **Velociraptor**, 3. **Stegosaurus**, 4. **Triceratops**, 5. **Spinosaurus**, 6. **Brachiosaurus**, 7. **Protoceratops.**

The illustrated dinosaur is a **Spinosaurus**.

PAGES 84–5

66 Diary of a knight

Some words may fit in more than one space. Here is one version:

My name is Lance Moat and I live with my family in an **incredibly** grand castle, and I'm training to be a **heroic** knight.

Read my diary to see what **exciting** things I got up to yesterday…

Monday 6th January, 1405

<u>Morning</u>

The day didn't start **brilliantly** as I slept in this cold, **glacial** morning so didn't have time for breakfast. Instead I swiped some **humongous** chunks of bread and cheese from the table as I **hurtled** past as fast as a galloping horse.

I was late for my arithmetic lesson and was **anxious** Mr Bodmass would be **furious** with me. But it wasn't so **horrendous**, as I managed to sneak in at the back, so I don't think Mr Bodmass noticed I was late.

<u>Afternoon</u>

There was just time for a brisk lunch of pottage (that's **watery** vegetable soup to you twenty-first century readers!) and a mug of **sweet** milk after my morning lessons. Then I spent the afternoon on horseback doing my favourite thing in the world: riding a horse at full speed, holding a **massive** lance and trying to spear rings on the tip of the lance. I'm practising with a blunt lance, but when I get older and become more **proficient** at it, I'll get to use an **official** sharp lance.

PAGE 86

Backwards and forwards

Peep, kay**a**k, so**l**os, c**i**vic, Han**n**ah, ra**d**ar, **r**otor, w**o**w, mada**m**, l**e**vel.

A **palindrome** is the name given to a word that reads the same backwards as forwards.

PAGE 87

Word ladder 3

1. **taste,** 2. **haste,** 3. **teach,** 4. **cheap,** 5. **chase,** 6. **crash,** 7. **chair,** 8. **China.**

PAGES 88–9

Cave code

Code: the **second** letter of the name of each animal is the letter it stands for.

The animals, and the letters they stand for, are: s**t**arfish, s**h**ark, p**e**nguin; o**s**trich, c**a**mel, p**u**ffin, o**s**trich, b**a**dger, i**g**uana, p**e**nguin.

The cave painting message reads: **The sausage!**

Teacher: What came after the Stone Age?

Pupil: **The sausage**!

PAGE 90

70 Hunt the homophones

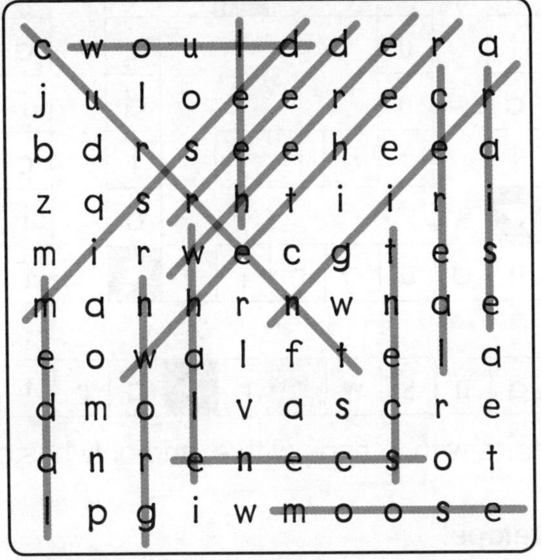

The homophones are: currant – **current**, mist – **missed**, read – **reed**, weather – **whether**, heal – **heel**, rein – **reign**, sent – **scent**, wear – **where**, groan – **grown**, mousse – **moose**, seen – **scene**, wail – **whale**, meddle – **medal**, rays – **raise**, serial – **cereal**, wood – **would**.

PAGE 91

Antonym antics

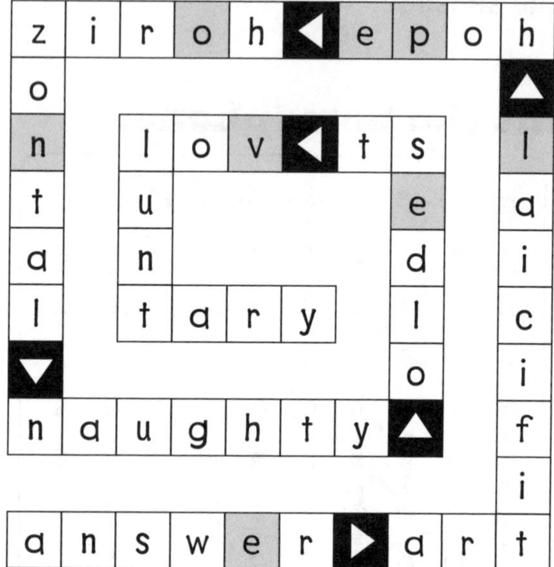

What starts with e, ends with e, and only has one letter?

An **envelope**!

PAGES 92–3

Quick quiz 2

1. **A** **Compulsory** is an antonym of voluntary, as it means the opposite.

2. **R** **Primarily** is a synonym of firstly, as it has a similar meaning.

3. **C** **Whether** is a homophone for weather, as both words sound the same, but are spelt differently, with different meanings.

4. **H** The unscrambled word **a l t c t e r** is **clatter**, which is a loud word. The other word r p e w h s i, is whisper, which is a quiet word.

5. **E** **Gnat**.

6. **R** **Obedient**, as all the words end in ent.

7. **F** Every second letter spells out **disgusting**.

8. **I** **Level**.

9. **S** **Parent**.

10. **H** **Bold**.

The underwater creature is an **archerfish**.

An archerfish has amazing talents, as it has an unusual way of catching its prey. It shoots a jet of water at small lizards and insects living on land and knocks them into the water. It can also jump out of the water to catch its prey. Archerfish live in countries such as Australia and India.

PAGE 96

What comes next 2?

These words are all modal auxiliary verbs. Other modal auxiliary verbs are: **could, might, should, will**. Modal auxiliary verbs cannot be used on their own. They are used with action verbs for example, "I **might win** the race."

PAGE 97

Guess the letter 2

1. The 12th consonant is **p**, 2. Advance eight letters to **x**, 3. The antonym of smooth is **rough**. Retreat 5 letters to **s**, 4. Retreat 5 letters to **n**, 5. Continue back to the next symmetrical letter **m**, 6. A synonym of zero is **nought**. Go forwards 2 to **o**.

You start at **p** and end at **o**.

PAGES 98–9

Moon munchies

Teacher: 5. I'll give you ten team points if you give me olives for a starter. Did you know that an olive tree can live up to 600 years?

Scientist: 2. I'll have 500 millilitres of the tomato soup boiled to 100°C, and mixed with 100 grams of bread.

Comedian: 4. Vanilla ice cream with raspberry sauce and cashew nuts please. I say, what did the nut say when it sneezed? Cashew!

Writer: 6. Some succulent steak with crunchy hand-cut chips. Please can the chips be as crisp as autumnal leaves and the steak seasoned with a delicate hint of exotic pepper.

Politician: 1. The fruit grown here on the Moon is the most environmentally friendly. Wouldn't you agree? But the vegetables are equally good.

Police officer: 3. Code seven. Salad. Over. Suspects include iceberg lettuce, tuna, cherry tomatoes, green beans and dressing. Confirm.

PAGE 100

76 Missing creatures 1

1. kn**owl**edge, pr**owl**, wildf**owl**, 2. **goose**berry, **goose**bumps, mon**goose**, 3. **fish**monger, jelly**fish**, sel**fish**, 4. **fox**glove, **fox**trot, out**fox**.

PAGE 101

77 Word sandwiches 3

1. suit**case**, **case**book, 2. country**side, side**show, 3. stereo**type, type**writer, 4. spot**light, light**house, 5. un**earth, earth**quake, 6. shell**fish, fish**tail, 7. road**show, show**case, 8. road**side, side**line, 9. sand**paper, paper**weight, 10. under**stand, stand**by.

PAGE 102

78 Word square 3

Here are some of the words of four or more letters you can make out of the letters u, v, l, o, t, r, e, n, e:

Four-letter words: **note, lent, lout, runt, teen, tone, tore, torn, tour, tree, true, tune, turn, vent, veto, vote**

Five-letter words: **enter, event, outer, toner, voter**

Six-letter words: **neuter, relent, revolt, tureen**

Nine-letter words: **volunteer**

Did you spot the nine-letter word? Well done if you did, and if you found any other words.

PAGE 103

79 The biggest picture

1. Have **your nose in a book**. 2. Don't **cry over spilt milk**. 3. A **little bird told me**. 4. A **picture** paints **a thousand words**.

PAGE 104

80 Odd one out 1

Group 1: **quietly** is the odd one out because all the other words in the group are adverbs of time, showing **when** or **how often** something is happening. Quietly is an adverb, but it's an adverb that describes how something is performed, and is not an adverb of time.

Group 2: **tomorrow** is the odd one out because all the other words in the group are adverbs of place, showing **where** something is happening. Tomorrow is an adverb, but it's an adverb that describes when something is happening, and is not an adverb of place.

Group 3: **beside** is the odd one out because all the other words in the group are adverbs of manner, describing **how** something is performed. Beside is an adverb, but it's an adverb that describes where something is performed, and is not an adverb of manner.

PAGE 105

Guess the word 4

Shield **H** belongs to Sir Laughalot, as the word is **comfortable**.

PAGES 106–7

Wacky weather

1. **cloudy**, 2. **Celsius**, 3. **drizzle**, 4. **rainbow**, 5. **tornado**, 6. **tsunami**, 7. **blizzard**, 8. **hurricane**, 9. **lightning**, 10. **thunderstorm**.

What's the difference between the weather and the climate?

You can't weather a tree, but you can climate!

This is a pun on the words *climb it*!

PAGE 108

Missing letters

Group 1: han**d**some, Feb**r**uary, **a**isle, wei**g**h, le**o**pard, solem**n**.

Group 2: g**u**itar, autum**n**, kni**t**, s**c**issors, t**o**ugh, gua**r**d, hym**n**.

Group 3: **m**nemonic, pe**o**ple, g**u**ess, i**s**land, lov**e**.

The three words are **dragon**, **unicorn** and **mouse**. The odd word out is **mouse** because it's a real animal and the other two creatures are mythical, or because it's small and the other two creatures are big.

PAGE 109

The Daily Rant

Some words can be used in more than one place. As long as the report makes sense, the words are correct. Check in a dictionary if you are unsure about a definition.

Here is what you could have written: You will never see such a beautiful sight as a herd of **elegant elephants** striding across the African savannah. It is **important** to value these magnificent **giants** whose future is threatened by poaching and destruction of their habitat. And it's **arrogant** and **ignorant** to assume these **exuberant** beasts will live forever, as in an **instant** they may be gone.

PAGE 110

What comes next 3?

These verbs are all the simple past tense of irregular verbs: **began – begin, broke – break, chose – choose, taught – teach, bought – buy, drank – drink, ate – eat, froze – freeze, spoke – speak**. Any word that is the simple past tense of an irregular verb is correct here for example: caught, crept, got, hung, laid and saw.

PAGE 111

86 Gift of the gab

n	u	o	s	k	c	o	s	r	e
d									d
o						e	y		l
u							e		u
b							n		o
t							i		h
r							v		s
e	e	g	g	r	a	p	e		t
									h
b	o	n	n	e	t	h	o	u	g

PAGE 112

87 Marvellous mnemonics

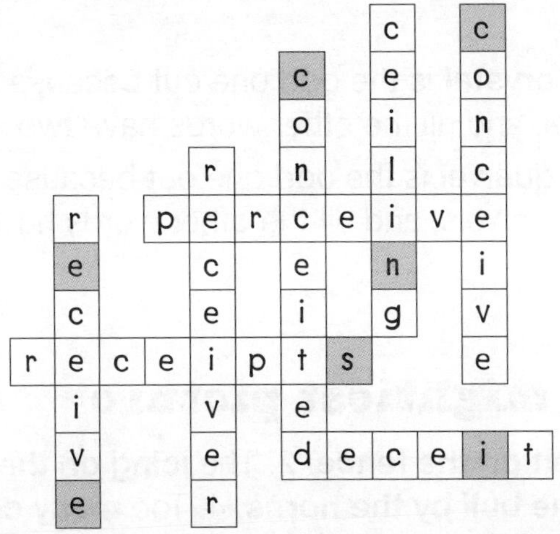

An exception to the rule i before e except after c is the word **science**.

PAGE 113

Word-eating machine

Here are some of the words with four or more letters that you can make out of letters in the word **experiment**:

Four-letter words: **rent, teen, term, tier, time, tree, trim, trip, pert, pier, meet, mere, mint, next, peer, perm, prim**

Five-letter words: **mixer, prime, print, timer**

Six-letter words: **expert, permit**

Seven-letter word: **extreme**

Well done if you found any others.

PAGE 114

Odd one out 2

Group 1: **vehicle** is the odd one out because it has three vowels, and all the other words have two vowels.

Group 2: **crystal** is the odd one out because it has one vowel, and all the other words have two vowels.

Group 3: **quarrel** is the odd one out because it has three vowels, and all the other words have two vowels.

PAGE 115

The mightiest picture

1. Don't **sit on the fence**. 2. The **icing on the cake**. 3. Take **the bull by the horns**. 4. Too **many cooks spoil the broth**.

PAGE 116

91 Word pyramid 3

1. **ant**, 2. **pant**, 3. **slant**, 4. **vacant**, 5. **currant**, 6. **dominant**, 7. **deodorant**, 8. **restaurant**.

PAGE 117

92 Picture this 3

1. **disguise**, 2, **embarrassed**, 3. **graffiti**, 4. **jewellery**, 5. **leopard**, 6. **yacht**.

Tricky words are words that aren't spelt as they sound, so other tricky words you could illustrate include: tongue, twelfth, soldier, beautiful and ocean.

PAGE 118

93 Missing creatures 2

1. butter**fly**, **fly**away, **fly**-past, 2. **bird**'s-eye, **bird**watching, lady**bird**, 3. s**cow**l, **cow**ard, **cow**boy, 4. cari**cat**ure, **cat**alogue, de**cat**hlon.

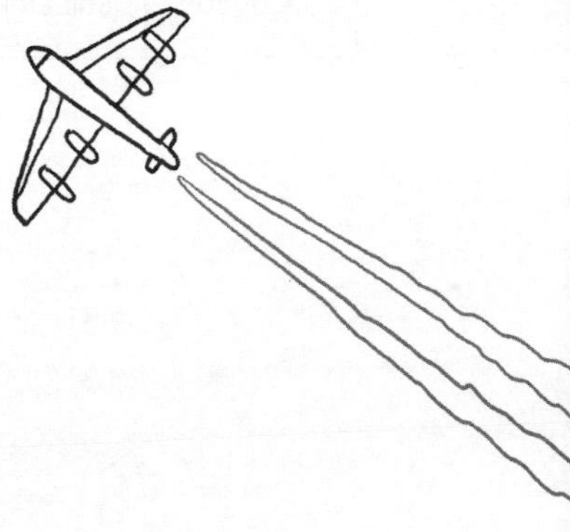

PAGE 119

Treasure trail

treat	champion	tortoise	treasure
trouble	ceiling	treacle	treason
toffee	tongue	tonsils	tighten
tempting	territory	tango	beautiful
tentacle	terrible	tangle	furniture
temptation	tantrum	musician	temple
temporary	temperature	temper	tadpole
tarragon	technique	television	tasteful
teaspoon	technology	telegraph	teacher
Tabitha	something	somewhere	stampede

PAGE 120

95 What comes next 4?

Did you spot the sequence? Each word has one fewer vowel than the previous word: **onomatopoeia** (8 vowels); **responsibilities** (7 vowels); **radioactive** (6 vowels); **silhouette** (5 vowels); **Hawaii** (4 vowels); **quiet** (3 vowels); **solemn** (2 vowels). Therefore, any word with 1 vowel (such as cycl**e**, th**ir**ty, br**a**nch, tw**e**lfth), and then any word with no vowels (such as gym, myth, hymn, lynx) continues the sequence.

PAGE 121

96 Feeding time

The four- and five-letter words you may have found include:

Five-letter words: **spoon, noose, snoop, snout, spent, spout, stone, stoop.**
Well done if you found some others.

Four-letter words: **oops, anon, east, nape, nest, noon, note, pant, pass, peat, pest, post, pout, punt, puss, seat, sent, soon, soup, spot, spun, step, stop, tape, tone, toss, tune**.
Well done if you found some others.

PAGES 122–3

Seeing double

1. **bitter**, 2. **course**, 3. **crane**, 4. **crust**, 5. **lash**, 6. **letter**, 7. **pupil**, 8. **snake**, 9. **stable**, 10. **tense**.

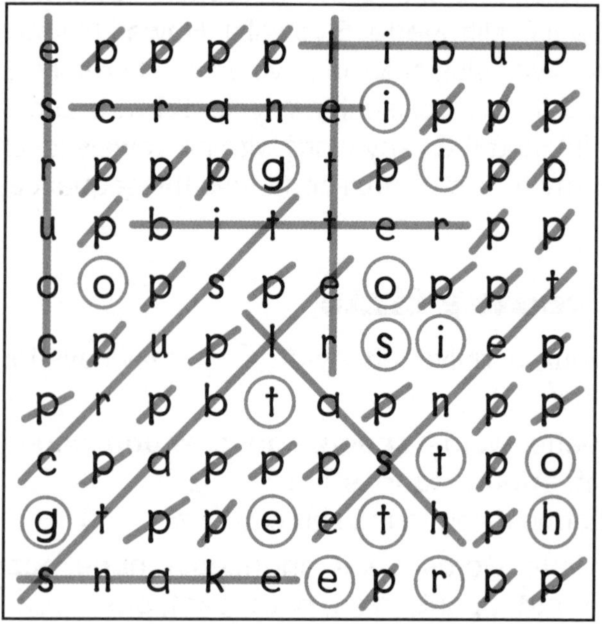

How does a penguin build its home?

Igloos it together!

PAGE 124

98 Crossword challenge 2

	1 m		2 a	n	x	i	o	u	3 s
	e		l						u
	4 d	e	l	i	5 c	i	6 o	u	s
	i		o		a		b		p
	7 c	o	w	a	r	d	s		i
	i				r		e		c
8 e	n	o	9 r	m	o	u	s		i
	e		i		t		s		o
			o						u
10 f	i	c	t	i	t	i	o	u	s

What do you call a fake noodle?

An **impasta!**

PAGE 125

99 McFlannery's flyshoes

MCFLANNERY'S FLYSHOES – THERE'S NO BETTER WAY TO TRAVEL!

Does it take you a **million** hours to travel to school?

Are you tired of sitting at the back of the school bus, in **massive** traffic queues?

Or does the walk to school seem to get **longer** every day?

Well, now you can leave all that hassle behind and literally take off with a pair of McFlannery's **fantastic** Flyshoes!

Simply slide your feet into the shoes, clip the buckles, flick the switch... and be prepared for the **ride of your life**!

These hassle-free Flyshoes are so easy to look after. Just plug them into a **charging** point after every ten hours of use.

And priced at only £99 a pair, they're the bargain of the **century**!

Hurry and order your Flyshoes **immediately** before they're sold out!

PAGE 126

Double trouble

1. **h**and; 2. **o**range; 3. **m**ean; 4. **o**bject; 5. **n**egative; 6. **y**ak; 7. **m**ood.

A **homonym** is a word that has two meanings.

PAGE 127

Blast off!

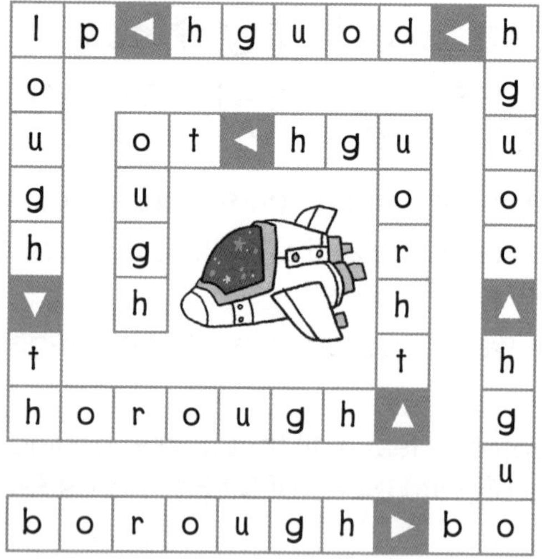

PAGES 128–9

102 Pupil super sleuth

The message reads:

To all teachers,

According to a myth, a hairy, toothless beast patrols the school at night. I dismissed the story, until the caretaker found some enormous muddy footprints that don't belong to anything from Earth.

The police are making this a priority. Keep this secret and don't panic!

Miss Prim,

Headmistress

The pattern for the code is all the letters in alphabetical order are numbered from 1 to 26, starting at 'f', so:

a = 22, b = 23, c = 24, d = 25, e = 26, f = 1, g = 2, h = 3, i = 4, j = 5, k = 6, l = 7, m = 8, n = 9, o = 10, p = 11, q = 12, r = 13, s = 14, t = 15, u = 16, v = 17, w = 18, x = 19, y = 20, z = 21.

PAGES 130–1

Super sport

1a. rhubar**b**, b. **b**elieve, 2a. dilemm**a**, b. **a**pplaud, 3a. beache**s**, b. **s**pecial, 4a. hammoc**k**, b. **k**nuckle, 5a. measur**e**, b. **e**vening, 6a. though**t**, b. **t**ension, 7a. distur**b**, b. **b**ecause, 8a. formul**a**, b. **a**ddress, 9a. initia**l**, b. **l**uggage, 10a. magica**l**, b. **l**ullaby.

Daisy's sport is wheelchair **basketball**.

PAGE 132

Odd one out 3

Group 1: **official** is the odd one out because the last letter of each other word follows in alphabetical order from a to h: encyclopedia, honeycomb, magnetic, reserved, preference, waterproof, boomerang, strength.

Group 2: **prestigious** is the odd one out because the last letter of each other word follows in alphabetical order from h to o: commonwealth, spaghetti, hajj, landmark, multicultural, criticism, solemn, armadillo.

Group 3: **circumference** is the odd one out because the last letter of each other word follows in alphabetical order from r to y: spectacular, suspicious, independent, menu, satnav, interview, archaeopteryx, compulsory.

PAGE 133

Crossword challenge 3

What stays in the corner, yet travels all over the world?

A stamp!

PAGES 134–5

06 Top secret

1. **special**, 2. **confidential**, 3. **artificial**,
4. **credentials**, 5. **beneficial**, 6. **initial**,
7. **essential**, 8. **impartial**, 9. **providential**,
10. **potential**, 11. **torrential**.

What do you get when you cross a computer with a lifeguard?

A **screensaver!**

PAGES 136–7

07 Sound twins

p	r	o	p	h	e	c	y		
r			r				o		
o			i				u	r	n
c			n			l			
e			c			i		h	
e		l	i	c	e	n	c	e	
d			p			k		r	
			l			s	i	d	e
	g	u	e	s	t				
					o	w	e	d	

PAGES 138–9

108 Whopping word search

1. **autumn**, 2. **campaign**, 3. **exhibition**, 4. **exhilarate**, 5. **ghost**, 6. **ghoul**, 7. **gnome**, 8. **hour**, 9. **knee**, 10. **knight**, 11. **knot**, 12. **limbs**, 13. **neigh**, 14. **pneumonia**, 15. **pteranodon**, 16. **rhythm**, 17. **two**, 18. **whale**.

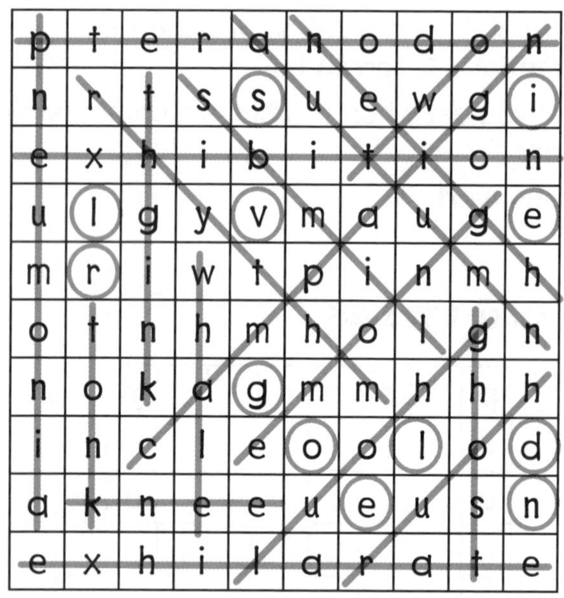

Speech is **silver**, but silence is **golden**.

PAGES 140–1

Quick quiz 3

1. **T** **Thoughtful**.
2. **R** The expression is **barking up the wrong tree**.
3. **U** **Cheap** is an antonym of expensive, as it means the opposite.

4. **F** **Terrible**.
5. **F** **Guessed** (past tense verb, meaning to have given an answer when you were not sure).
6. **L** The letter **n**.
7. **E** **Nought**.
8. **D** A **selfish** person doesn't think of others.
9. **O** **Outside**, which is an adverb of place, like upstairs and everywhere. Yesterday is an adverb of time.
10. **G** The expression is: **A picture paints a thousand words**.

The animal is a **truffle dog**.

A truffle dog is the name of a dog that has been trained to hunt for truffles. A truffle is an underground fungus that is a delicacy in restaurants. A truffle was once sold for £165,000! But truffles are hard to find as they grow underground, and if they're not picked when they're just ripe, they're worthless. Originally an Italian dog, called a lagotto romagnolo, was trained to hunt for truffles, but now other dogs are also trained. They sniff out where the truffles are buried and paw at the spot.

Notepad

Notepad

Notepad